D1237461

MASS MEDIA
AND THE
NATIONAL
EXPERIENCE

MASS MEDIA AND THE NATIONAL EXPERIENCE

ESSAYS IN COMMUNICATIONS HISTORY

Edited by
Ronald T. Farrar
Southern Methodist University
and
John D. Stevens
University of Michigan

Harper & Row, Publishers
New York, Evanston, San Francisco, London

FOR GAYLA AND JO

CONTENTS

PREFACE

It is all too easy for those in any academic or professional field to become so absorbed in the tasks immediately before them that they lose sight of where they have been and where they might be going. Historians, whose business is to put developments in perspective, are as prone to this malady as anyone else. This collection of original essays is an attempt to allow journalism historians to reflect on the present state of their art, and to suggest ways and means of doing the important work that lies ahead. It is the first unified attempt to bring together such observations, and, as such, might prove a milestone by which future generations can gauge their progress.

We spent nearly three years in assigning, coordinating, and gathering these chapters, but each essay carries the personal stamp of the man who wrote it. His assertions are his own; our final editorial changes in most chapters were minimal.

The purpose of this book is to suggest productive areas of research for students, faculty, professional journalists, and all others interested in the history of mass communications. If the book does this, it will have more than justified the effort which went into it.

Ronald T. Farrar
John D. Stevens

MASS MEDIA
AND THE
NATIONAL
EXPERIENCE

1 MASS COMMUNICATIONS HISTORY: A MYRIAD OF APPROACHES

Ronald T. Farrar

Ronald T. Farrar is chairman of the Department of Journalism at Southern Methodist University and winner of the 1969 Sigma Delta Chi award for research in journalism for his biography of Charles G. Ross, *Reluctant Servant.*

In 1810, in the declining years of an extraordinary life, Isaiah Thomas decided to piece together, for the first time, the history of journalism in America. He had some misgivings about his task, and said so:

> I am sensible that a work of this kind might, in other hands, have been rendered more interesting. It has a long time been the wish of many that some person distinguished for literature would bring it forward; but as no one has appeared who was

disposed to render this service to the republic of letters . . . I
have been, perhaps too easily, led to engage in a task which has
proved more arduous than I had previously apprehended, and
which has been attended with much expense.[1]

Isaiah Thomas possessed more talent, money, and energy than
most men, and he was able to surmount difficulties that would have
dissuaded less determined scholars. His two-volume *History of
Printing in America* stood alone for 60 years. Since that time, however, more than a dozen other intrepid souls have reconstructed the
pioneering work of Isaiah Thomas, brought the evolution of journalism in America more nearly up to date, and contributed their
own interpretations in their own way. The variety now ranges from
The Newspaper and Periodical Press, by S. N. D. North, who
primly refrained from describing the colorful personalities of journalism's great writers and editors, to the lively and readable *Makers
of Modern Journalism,* by Kenneth Stewart and John Tebbel, whose
approach was purely biographical; from Bernard A. Weisberger's
The American Newspaperman, written with the cool detachment
of the professional historian who happened to be interested in journalism, to *The Development of American Journalism,* by Sidney
Kobre, a journalism professor who happened to be interested in
history; from Alfred M. Lee's *The Daily Newspaper in America,* a
dispassionate sociological treatise, to Frederic Hudson's *Journalism
in the United States,* dedicated to "The Press: The Argus of the
World, The Ear-Gallery of the Globe, The Reporter of the Universe."

Even at that, the output is surprisingly small—particularly in
view of the close similarity, in intellectual spirit and in method,
between history and journalism. Only two volumes in recent years
have come close to combining thoroughgoing scholarship with read-
ability: *American Journalism,* by Frank Luther Mott, and *The
Press and America,* by Edwin Emery and Henry Ladd Smith.[2] But

[1]Isaiah Thomas, *The History of Printing in America, with a Biography of
Printers and an Account of Newspapers* (Worcester, Mass., 1810), p. 3.
Thomas's expenses included the purchase of back files of many early news-
papers; these cost him about $1000, but proved invaluable to later scholars.

[2]Emery and Smith combined on the original edition of *The Press and
America* (Englewood Cliffs, N.J., 1954). Professor Smith wrote the first
portion of the book, which is essentially unchanged in the revised edition of
1962. This edition carries Professor Emery's name alone.

for all the enormity and brilliance of his contribution, Mott inexplicably wrote journalism history as an end in itself, all but isolated from the larger context—American and world history as a whole—in which the story of journalism perforce must be examined. Emery and Smith did take considerable trouble to emphasize political, social, and economic trends as they affected journalism history, but their book contains a built-in generation gap. As pointed out by an Indiana University graduate student, Donald Oehlerts,[3] Emery and Smith depended for their interpretations of American history exclusively upon the writings of men popular in their own university years. The sources include such giants of progressive history as Charles A. Beard, Frederick Jackson Turner, and Vernon Parrington, along with Claude Bowers, Arthur M. Schlesinger, Sr., John D. Hicks, and Allan Nevins—formidable figures all, but scarcely representative of the full scope of present-day historical thought. Oehlerts's painstaking analysis of footnotes and bibliography in all the current general works of journalism history produced no evidence whatever of the searching reexamination posed in the last 20 years by Daniel Boorstin, Louis Hartz, Richard Hofstadter, David Potter, William Appleman Williams, and Henry Nash Smith, nor of any of the hundreds of books, monographs, papers, and journal articles which have challenged and tested almost every period of history in almost every region of the country. In short, an entire generation of American scholars—a profoundly important one, and by all odds the largest—has slipped unnoticed by the pages of journalism history.

This book is a modest attempt at beginning the repair of that imbalance. The essays that follow, written exclusively for these pages, reflect some of current scholarship's suggestions for rediscovering the common ground between the history of mass communications and the history of the country. It was not possible, or even desirable, to attempt full chronological or thematic coverage. Each essayist was asked to be indicative rather than definitive. If there is a common theme, it is merely that much work needs to be done.

•   •   •

[3]Donald E. Oehlerts, "The Influence of Interpretations of American History on the History of the Press" (Paper presented to the Association for Education in Journalism, Berkeley, Calif., 1969).

While the previous chronicles of American journalism are for one reason or another vulnerable, the wonder remains—given the complexities of the subject matter and the environment the journalism historian typically has had to occupy—that they exist at all. The nation's "press" includes such poles of excellence as the *National Observer* and the *National Enquirer;* it includes, too, the *Reader's Digest* and the *East Village Other,* and whatever falls in between. "Not a few precious scoundrels mix with the high-minded editors in these pages," Mott warns the readers of his *American Journalism.* "There is ridiculous clowning along with serious performance. . . . The careful student of newspapers and newspapermen finds so wide a difference between the best and worst of them that he accepts the epigram that the only safe generalization about journalism is that no generalization about it is safe."[4] Even the story of a single, carefully selected publication can present overwhelming obstacles, as Allan Nevins, distinguished both in journalism and in history, points out:

> Compare the task of the biographer of a newspaper with that of the biographer of such a public figure as William Jennings Bryan. The author of a life of Bryan has to relate him to the history of his times—and ours; but only to the history of politics, for apart from a few unhappy episodes like his enlistment in the battle of fundamentalism against evolution, Bryan was merely a political animal; and even in politics only a restricted number of issues, of which currency and imperialism were the chief, need be considered. But the man who writes the history of a great newspaper for the same period has to take cognizance of a thousand subjects, from the poetry corner to corners in wheat. If he does not fix on the right principles of selection and synthesis, he might as well throw himself into the nearest vat of printer's ink.[5]

Compounding the problem, to the frustration of Nevins and others who have attempted to reconstruct journalism's past, is the newspaperman's all-too-common lack of a sense of history—a professional obligation to organize private notes, diaries of editorial conferences, confidential staff directives, correspondence, and other memorabilia

---

[4] Frank Luther Mott, *American Journalism* (New York, 1962), p. vii.

[5] Allan Nevins, "American Journalism and Its Historical Treatment," *Journalism Quarterly* 36:4 (Fall 1959), 413.

into an archive which could someday be used to piece together the story behind the story. Typically, the secret history of an important article or editorial is not committed to paper; such documents of inside history as do exist—background notes, intraoffice memoranda—are seldom filed. This forces the historian to rely on the treacherously uncertain recollections of the persons involved—often years afterward—and on the story as it actually appeared in print. "Here," a famous managing editor once bellowed to his staff as he pointed to an item in his newspaper, "is a lie. I know it is a lie, but I must print it because it is spoken by a prominent public official. The public official's name and position make the lie news. . . . Printing these lies . . . is one of the hardest things I have to do."[6] Arthur M. Schlesinger, Jr., who interrupted a remarkable career as an historian to become an advisor to President John F. Kennedy, emerged from the White House with his confidence in journalism permanently shaken:

> As for newspaper or magazine accounts, they are sometimes worse than useless when they purport to give the inside reality of decisions; their relation to reality is often considerably less than the shadows in Plato's cave. I have too often seen the most conscientious reporters attribute to government officials views the exact opposite of which the officials were advocating within the government to make it possible for me to take the testimony of journalism in such matters seriously again.[7]

Schlesinger admitted he himself had deliberately misinformed the press on at least one occasion; he apologized for it,[8] doubtless to the chagrin of his colleagues in the White House. Governments, from Julius Caesar's time to Schlesinger's, have resolutely tried to manage the news—by outright lies if the need arose, as it often seems to have—and reporters and editors who are "managed" usually perceive that they're being had. If half-truths or untruths do get into print, they usually do so in the name of objective reporting—which is alternately praised and damned as the great strength/

---

[6]James Markham, *Bovard of the Post-Dispatch* (Baton Rouge, La., 1954), p. 147.

[7]Arthur M. Schlesinger, Jr., "The Historian and History," *Foreign Affairs* 41:3 (April 1963), p. 493.

[8]William H. Taft, *Newspapers as Tools for Historians* (Columbia, Mo., 1970), p. 121.

weakness of American journalism. But the same editors who do publish suspicious statements could, for the ultimate record, explain their doubts in memoranda which might be safely tucked away in the newspaper's archive to assist some future historian in getting at the truth.

Few such archives now exist. One is at the *Post-Dispatch.* Because he was so very nearly blind, Joseph Pulitzer II spent much of his professional life away from the newspaper he loved; on doctor's orders he combined the relaxation of travel with the controlled rigors of outdoor life. No matter where Pulitzer happened to be, however, he remained in constant and knowing touch with his headquarters in St. Louis. Secretaries—men of rare skill in the arts of selection and condensation—would read to him by the hour, then write down the dozens of comments and instructions Pulitzer dictated for his reporters, editors, and managers. These documents, carefully catalogued, provide splendid insights into the history of a great newspaper and the region and the country it served. They are not now generally available to historians, but perhaps in time they will be. Many other newspapers, magazines, and broadcast news operations have similar contributions to make to historical understanding through archives of their own, should they be inclined to maintain them.

Similarly *verboten* to historians are records from the business offices. Only the merest handful of the nation's newspapers, magazines, and broadcasters choose to make public reports from their counting rooms—this despite the fact that the essentially private nature of American mass media often presupposes that editorial and commercial success can be synonymous. If one believes, with the elder Pulitzer, that only a financially sound press can be trusted to withstand outside economic pressures and maintain its editorial integrity and independence, then the figures on the balance sheets are worth studying by historians. The essay by William Ames and Dwight Teeter in this collection provides convincing proof of the value of financial information in describing media growth and understanding media performance.

The business office might also contribute in another way to the writing of journalism history—that is, by refusing to commission the righteous, self-serving, and hotly promoted works of commemoration that pass for the "history" of far too many newspaper, wire service, and magazine operations. Such smug efforts not only result in distortions, but they also tend to discourage less partisan studies on the grounds that the subject has already been "done."

Often, of course, the glossing over of harsh truths in journalism history is not done on orders of a publisher or business manager, but on the writer's own outsized sense of responsibility. The journalist might think of himself as the last of the world's free spirits; then he is asked to write the history of his own newspaper, and right away he becomes a protective sentimentalist. In what is perhaps the most absorbing narrative history of American journalism, written 50 years ago by George Henry Payne, there is this sample:

> At an engagement near Santiago, Cuba, just previous to the battle of El Caney, in the Spanish-American War, there was a correspondent named Edward Marshall, of the New York *Journal*. He was where, if he had due regard for his own life, he would not have been—in the front with the soldiers. A bullet struck his thigh, making him a cripple for life; as he lay bleeding and wounded—how seriously, it was not possible to tell—he dictated to a comrade his story for his paper. It was foolhardy, as someone afterward suggested,—but was it not also magnificent?[9]

For his skill at gathering and reporting such poignant episodes as this, however, Payne cannot be excused for ducking as he did such larger questions as the blame the wounded reporter's own publisher—William Randolph Hearst—should share for that war's ever happening in the first place. Many reporters are too in love with newspapers to give their history the tough-minded judgment it ought to have. Nevins, for one, thinks the writing job might be better done by a college professor:

> A [history] writer selected within the [newspaper] office, and particularly in the newsroom, will be more expert than an outsider; an outsider will be more objective. The advice of a good college or university department of history can be obtained more readily than most newspapermen suppose, and will be more valuable than they generally believe. University teachers write badly, but they have a sense of organization, and they will see aspects of the subject that newspapermen may miss.[10]

[9]George Henry Payne, *History of Journalism in the United States* (New York, 1920), p. 380.

[10]Nevins, *op. cit.*, p. 422.

The suggestion that college professors may be more temperamentally (if not artistically) suited to write journalism history makes sense, and, indeed, within the academic community the schools and departments of journalism have claimed from their beginning to be vitally concerned with the teaching and writing of history. The first course ever to meet in the world's first school of journalism was "The History and Principles of Journalism," and the dean of the school, Walter Williams, taught it personally. A man of enormous presence, who later became president of the University of Missouri—the fact that he himself had never done so much as a semester's college work was dismissed as a mere technicality—Williams was a fiery and extraordinarily gifted lecturer. The History and Principles course turned hundreds of idealistic, uncommitted students into journalism majors, and Williams's oratory, perhaps as much as anything else, was responsible for the success of the journalism school experiment. Williams's pattern was widely copied around the country, almost always by less talented men, and can be found even today, more than 60 years later. But if inspirational history produced some dedicated young journalists, it also produced little in the way of honest scholarship. Far too often, the journalism historian came to be regarded by colleagues in other academic disciplines as an unthinking apologist for journalism, and by professionals in the field of journalism regarded not at all. Indeed, the slashing commentaries on present-day media operations coming from such diverse personages as Spiro T. Agnew and Marshall McLuhan might have caused fewer shock waves if journalism historians, who know better, had been more outspoken in the first place. A perceptive young historian, Elizabeth L. Eisenstein, points out what can occur when those who should do their scholarly duty don't.

> Where historians are prone to be overcautious, others are encouraged to be overbold. Evasion on the part of careful scholars has, by default, allowed the topic to fall into more careless hands. The fifteenth-century "media revolution" is also of interest to those who cultivate various *avant-garde* fields (communications theory, media analysis, and the like) and who scrutinize the current scene without paying much heed to the past. Nonhistorians of this sort, however, are almost certain to go astray if they try to take short cuts on their own. In *The Gutenberg Galaxy* Mc-

Luhan provides a good case in point. The author has solved his difficulties by the simple, albeit inelegant, device of dispensing with chronological sequence and historical context altogether. Far from appearing to be concerned about preserving proportion and perspective, he impatiently brushes aside all such concerns as obsolete. Developments that spanned the course of five hundred years, affecting different regions and penetrating to different social strata at different levels, are randomly intermingled and treated as a single event—most appropriately described, perhaps, as a "happening."[11]

If thoughtful students of communications history are not yet prepared to accept the galloping theses of a Marshall McLuhan, then it is high time for them to produce explanations—less extravagant, obviously, but more plausible—of their own. Several signs exist that such work is at last underway.

•   •   •

One encouraging note is the interest recently shown in the field by scholars who normally concern themselves with other disciplines. Leonard W. Levy of Brandeis, Elmer E. Cornwell, Jr., of Brown, and George Juergens of Indiana University, as examples, have no formal affiliation with journalism but nevertheless tackled such important themes as the evolution of freedom of expression, national leadership and public opinion, and the Presidency and the press, respectively. Biographical studies, which have always been appealing to journalists—there are almost as many books about Horace Greeley, for instance, as there are general histories of journalism—have been ably done by such free-lance writers as William A. Swanberg and Richard O'Connor. Swanberg's deeply analytical biographies of Hearst and Pulitzer should be read by everyone in journalism and most persons outside it, and O'Connor's lively account, *The Scandalous Mr. Bennett,* provides keen insights into one of history's most disastrous and wretched publishing careers. Alexander Kendrick of CBS has written a sensitive biography of Edward R. Murrow. Personal memoirs by journalists and ex-journalists are providing at least partial explanations of such national in-

[11]Elizabeth L. Eisenstein, "The Advent of Printing in Current Historical Literature: Notes and Comment on an Elusive Transformation," *American Historical Review* 75:3 (February 1970), p. 742.

stitutions as *The New York Times,* Time, Inc., and the late
Saturday Evening Post.

Encouraging, too, are the less dramatic but equally useful articles
and monographs being generated by professors and advanced graduate students in the nation's schools and departments of journalism.
Where the history of journalism was once regarded as just another
subject—along with reporting, editing, and communications law—it
has lately been upgraded in many schools to something approaching
a legitimate area of concentration, deserving of more than a small
fraction of a man's time and energies. With specialization has come
a rising level of sophistication, clearly apparent not only at the
paper-presenting sessions of national conventions but—much more
importantly—in the classroom. On campus after campus, courses in
journalism history are attracting more and better students and gain-
ing in the esteem of faculty and colleagues in other disciplines. Graduate students in political science, speech, history, folklore, library
science, and other fields are being counseled to take seminars in
communications history. Interdisciplinary conferences, such as the
symposium on muckraking at Pennsylvania State University in the
spring of 1970, which brought together scholars from journalism,
American studies, and history, were proving the value of cross-
fertilization.

The pages of *Journalism Quarterly* represent another index to
current research trends in the field. In its earlier years, *Journalism
Quarterly* was a generous and easy outlet for essays in history; 57
percent of its total article space went to historical research in 1939,
52 percent in 1940. But some of these pieces were insular, many
more were poorly done, and there was not much protest when the
essays in history, like the traditionalists who wrote them, were
swept aside by the flood of behaviorists who came from out of
nowhere to revolutionize the field during the 1950s. Departments
of Journalism became Schools of Mass Communications, their new
faculty positions occupied by bright young Ph.D.'s with consuming
interests in quantification. Where the historian was concerned with
documents and style, the behaviorist was energetically counting,
measuring, surveying, experimenting—in short, the traditionalists
warned darkly—threatening to convert the warm and artful profession of journalism into a cold-blooded science. The same ideo-
logical conflict rocked other disciplines, too, notably political science

and geography, and generated some fierce academic infighting. In spite of the schism, or perhaps because of it, the behaviorists developed into enthusiastic and productive (if at times unintelligible) scholars, and their work permeated the literature. By 1954, only one historical essay, representing 2 percent of the available article space, appeared in *Journalism Quarterly,* and in 1955 the figure rose only to 7 percent. But the Darwinian struggle was not ended, and the historian as a species not yet extinct. Perhaps somewhat chastened to discover his previous work so expendable, he set forth with renewed determination to do more studies and do them better. By 1969, history accounted for 31 percent of the article space in *Journalism Quarterly,* and these essays tended to reflect more convincing scholarship. *The Journalism Monographs,* a promising if limited series begun in 1966 by the Association for Education in Journalism, has permitted several worthwhile studies, such as Carter R. Bryan's examination of early black newspapers in America, and Peter Knights's analysis of nineteenth-century newspaper competition, to get into print. Student research has improved; seminar papers that would have exhilarated a professor and dominated his class in 1960 were apt to be deemed routinely good ten years later. There were enough worthy seminar papers, in fact, to justify a national competition, with each year's prizewinner getting the Warren C. Price award for student research in communications history. For students and faculty alike, then, the field has taken on a new identity, a new sense of purpose, a new self-confidence, and a willingness to break new ground.

The essays in this book suggest the striking variety of interpretations and perspectives at work among those who are now teaching and writing the history of mass communications. Except for their comparative youth—the average age of the contributors is 40—and their extensive professional experience with the media, which journalism professors usually must acquire in addition to their doctorates, the men who wrote these pages have little in common. There is no single influence (although three of the contributors did study under one professor, Harold L. Nelson of Wisconsin) and no one point of view or unifying historical explanation in these chapters. Indeed, the editors feel an obligation to display the myriad of approaches being pursued by today's scholars. Thus we can find the social history approach of John M. Harrison alongside the economic interpretations of William Ames and Dwight Teeter; John Stevens's exploration of the new freedoms permitted by society and the courts contrasts with Donald Shaw's discussion of the freedoms permitted by technology. Richard Hixson and William Taft set forth the possibilities remaining in the neglected areas of regional and state studies, and Robert Thorp's chapter describes the methodological tools, training, and temperament needed by today's working historian.

The remaining essays delve into the important but little discussed matters of broadcast history, nonverbal communications, and black journalism. Each piece endeavors to suggest that a theme or a topic or even a period of history can be, as Lionel Trilling wrote in another connection, "freely touched and handled, picked up, turned over, looked at from this angle or that, and, at least in some sense, possessed."

•   •   •

Only tentative and fragmentary conclusions, of course, can be given. Perhaps this helps explain why the essays that follow possess a quiet sense of urgency unknown to scholars of other eras. These stirring times somehow forbid leisurely examination in the grand manner of the *New Yorker's* Eustace Tilley, who could amuse himself for hours by studying through his glass the movements of a captured butterfly. Instead we are surrounded—oppressed, as Theodore White insists[12]—by entire institutions which don't seem to work. Airlines, universities, medical care, government, the economy —all are buckling under the strain of today's needs. The media of mass communications are not merely the thermometer of this institutional illness; indeed, as an institution, perhaps the most visible and pervasive institution, the communications media are in deep trouble. Where Karl Marx once alleged to have found the driving force for revolution in the changes in means of production, Marshall McLuhan now claims to have detected it in changes in communications; the angry idealists who in one era directed their venom at Wall Street now reserve it for Madison Avenue. Bitter and contradictory accusations have today's journalism, and today's journal-

[12]Theodore White, "America's Two Cultures," *Columbia Journalism Review* 7:4 (Winter 1969–70), p. 12.

ists, either unresponsive or overly responsive to the exigencies of life in America. For all we know, both indictments could be true.

We cannot weigh or measure with precision the media's impact on the national mood, their responsibility for violence and coercion, or even what might be happening to us privately as a result of their intrusion into our personalities and spirits. But if the mass media have not succeeded—or if they have succeeded too well—then the fault is almost certainly with the institution rather than with the men who are its temporary custodians. Improving today's journalism is, in short, a task vastly more complex than replacing some reporters, editors, publishers, broadcasters, and producers. Instead, a thoroughgoing inquiry into the institution and all its phases is imperative, and the historical context must be far better described than it has been so far.

The past is, in its own way, fully as confusing, as complicated, and as fraught with contradictions as the present. Any historian who would presume to bring complete order and synthesis to the past—or to any portion thereof—must expect an unending series of crushing disappointments. Instead of illuminating his subject with one blinding revelation, he will probably have to settle for a handful of flickering insights—and the consolation that some light is far better than no light at all. The historian's success—making his light glow as brightly as possible—will come in direct proportion to the pertinence and importance of the questions he asks of the past, and the knowledge, judgment, and skill he commits to finding the answers. The communications historian, with special problems of his own, will rarely be able to reconstruct the past with utter certainty. Yet he must try, and he cannot throw away what truth he finds simply because it may not be the whole truth. For his judgments, in all their frailty, provide the only real basis for placing the triumphs and failures of the media of mass communications in honest and meaningful perspective.

Journalism's past, like the country's, is full of ambiguities, contradictions, and moments of soaring greatness. It is a past which must be continually ordered, examined, learned from. We hope this book will help.

FREEDOM OF EXPRESSION: NEW DIMENSIONS

John D. Stevens

John D. Stevens, University of Michigan, is chairman of the Research Committee of the History Division of the Association for Education in Journalism and a frequent contributor to *Journalism Quarterly* and other journals.

An old joke says that an optimist thinks a glass is half full of water while a pessimist thinks it is half empty. Approaching communications history in terms of freedom or restraint, from this viewpoint, long has interested journalism historians. It has been a recognized concept at least since the publication in 1952 of Fredrick S. Siebert's monumental study of the English press.[1]

[1]Fredrick S. Siebert, *Freedom of the Press in England 1476–1776* (Urbana, Ill., 1952).

In his introduction, Siebert suggested two "propositions" which he believed would hold for all societies and for all periods. Whether there is sufficient evidence within Siebert's own work to support these propositions can be argued; what cannot be disputed is their heuristic value. Since their publication, virtually every study of press freedom has hearkened to them.

Siebert's two propositions were:

> PROPOSITION I. *The extent of governmental control of the press depends on the nature of the relationship of the government to those subject to the government.*
>
> PROPOSITION II. *The area of freedom contracts and the enforcement of restraints increases as the stresses on the stability of the government and the structure of society increase.*

Siebert's second proposition, while often used by other scholars, still has untapped potential. Past studies have correlated some measures of intolerance (such as taxes, court convictions, or vigilante violence) with the turmoil in the country at that time. Siebert's study covered three centuries of English history. No other application covers that long a period, and it may be that the area of freedom contracts and expands too slowly for short-term measurement.[2]

Not to quibble with the wording of Siebert's second proposition, but it probably makes sense to insert "perceived" before "stresses" because in times of peril those involved always overestimate the danger. Another important consideration is that a crisis may goad the more brazen citizens—and bold citizens always are a tiny majority —to exercise their freedom. Such testing may have more lasting impact than the effects of a general contracting of freedom among the rest of the citizenry.

The history of American involvement in Korea and Vietnam suggests content analyses which could test the applicability of Siebert's

[2]E.g., Donald L. Shaw and Stephen W. Brauer, "Press Freedom and War Constraints: Case Testing Siebert's Proposition II," *Journalism Quarterly* 46:2 (Summer 1969), 243–254; John D. Stevens, "Press and Community Toleration: Wisconsin in World War I," *Journalism Quarterly* 46:2 (Summer 1969), 255–259.

propositions. In Korea, shifts in the fortunes of war could be traced as the United Nations troops moved up and down the peninsula; certainly it could be correlated with American press and public attitudes toward the conflict. Vietnam provides a longer-term study, one of increasing involvement and popular disillusionment with what appears to be an endless war. Throughout the late 1960s, the American media became more critical of the Vietnam War. Even some television commentators took antiwar positions, and broadcasters always have been less outspoken on political matters because of their vulnerability to direct congressional pressure. A society which will tolerate the kinds of criticisms published in the leftist-liberal publications and which will permit the performance of *MacBird* on Broadway or *Red, White and Maddox* in Atlanta has forgotten the definition of sedition, if indeed anyone ever knew it. Legal encyclopedia list dozens of definitions which courts have come up with, but most boil down to Mr. Justice Potter Stewart's conclusion about obscenity: "I know it when I see it." Any meaningful definition of freedom must include the freedom for any adult to purchase a ticket to *MacBird* and to make up his own mind about whether to panic if someone stands up and shouts "Fire!"

Siebert's propositions have served well, as they no doubt will continue to do. They are sequoias in a field overgrown with shrubs; however, it is time to plant some seedlings. We need more generalizations, even if those generalizations are chopped down by later researchers. American history certainly is richer for the generalizations by Charles Beard about economic determination among the framers of the Constitution and by Frederick Jackson Turner about the influence of the frontier, although no modern historian accepts either at face value. Neither does a modern journalism historian believe that John Peter Zenger's trial really changed American law or established the principle of freedom of the press. In truth, it had about as much impact on American law as the Boston Tea Party had on American etiquette. Political impact, yes; legal impact, no. Zenger still is important, even if he was a hired pawn in a chess game between powerful interests in New York.

Few scholars have attempted an historical overview of the American experience; fewer still have tried a synthesis of free expression theory.[3] Communications historians, like other historians, are reluctant to generalize. By nature and training they concentrate on the unique, while behaviorists tend to concentrate on the similarity of phenomena. Communications history has had no Beards or Turners, but in any scholarly field there is an implicit interest in seeking a unifying theory. Siebert-like propositions are necessary building blocks for such a communications theory, which when it emerges (perhaps generations from now) will almost certainly combine historical with so-called behavioral techniques and theories. Such cross-fertilization is not only desirable but probably inevitable.

This essay will suggest two major and several subsidiary hypotheses, or to use Siebert's term, propositions. In tribute to his pioneering work, these are numbered from where he stopped.

PROPOSITION III. *The more heterogeneous a society, the more freedom of expression it will tolerate.*

People do not "naturally" agree on much. If they do agree it is either because they have been forced to or (less frequently) because they share ideals. An agreement based on such shared values is not likely to endure without some element of coercion.

A society which either is tightly ruled or which shares values almost unanimously will not be friendly to expressions of dissent; it does not have to be. On the other hand, if there is not much centralized power, a society must try to avoid issues which will wreck its fragile coalition. In such a situation, a society has to endure some diversity of opinions.

For many periods of American history, little is known about the status of free expression—either in theory of the day or in what forms of dissent went unpunished. The manifest content of the publications is one indication, but content analysis only measures

[3]Former include Edward P. Cheyney, "Freedom and Restraint: A Short History," *Annals of the American Academy of Political Science* 200 (November 1938), 1–12, and Harold L. Nelson, *Freedom of the Press from Hamilton to the Warren Court* (Indianapolis, Ind., 1965). An example of the latter is Thomas I. Emerson, *Toward a General Theory of the First Amendment* (New York, 1967).

what is there; it does not get at what has been omitted. Most research attention has been focused on periods of war and war preparation, yet even this concentration has been spotty.

Journalism history has few books which can be considered "classics"; of these only four concentrate on freedom of the press, and all four cover the period before 1800. In addition to Siebert's work on England, they are Arthur M. Schlesinger, Sr., *Prelude to Independence: The Newspaper War on Britain* (1958); Leonard W. Levy, *Legacy of Suppression: Freedom of Speech in Early America* (1960), and James Morton Smith, *Freedom's Fetters: The Alien and Sedition Laws and American Civil Liberties* (1956).

Schlesinger documented the importance of colonial newspapers in unifying the colonies in their demands for political freedom. He also suggested that the Founding Fathers were more pragmatic than philosophical about free expression, a suggestion which Levy developed and popularized. Levy concluded that the framers of the Constitution had no idea what they were guaranteeing by the First Amendment beyond the right to publish without *prior* restraints, possible trial by jury, and reliance on truth as a defense for defendants in seditious libel cases. It was not until the Alien and Sedition Acts crisis (1798–1800) that the Jeffersonians recognized that procedural safeguards were not enough and came up with a philosophical underpinning for free expression.

Levy is not without his critics. One of the justified chastisements is that he devoted much more attention to the statute books and court records than he did to the contents of the colonial newspapers themselves. The rash of prosecutions under the Sedition Act did little to silence the Jeffersonian editors, even those under indictment.

Smith's book is both carefully researched and skillfully written. It analyzes all cases under the four laws known collectively as the Alien and Sedition Acts. Unfortunately, Smith has never published the companion volume on the Kentucky and Virginia Resolutions which he promised in the introduction to *Freedom's Fetters.*

Considering how much has been written about the Civil War, it is surprising that there has been no definitive study of its free expression aspects. The Spanish-American War, a war which cannot be separated from the journalism of the era, has fared better, as has World War I. World War II and later conflicts still are covered only in piecemeal fashion.[4]

John P. Roche has pointed out that American society was built on a myth of homogeneity which World War I shattered. There was a common assumption that somehow just becoming an American severed all of a man's previous loyalties. The ideal survived the nineteenth century because the United States—thanks mostly to the British fleet—was able to avoid entangling alliances. Each wave of immigrants waited for the Melting Pot to incorporate them, but such a goal depended on the continuation of an isolationist foreign policy and in 1915 and 1916 that policy became untenable. The United States was never neutral toward the war in Europe, in either thought or deed. It came as a terrible shock to the majority of Americans to see their German neighbors line up on the other side. The old American society which had been based on a bucolic, white Protestant heritage had been sapped by the new urban, industrial, Catholic, and immigrant explosion.[5]

Societies give up their myths hard, but the shattering of that homogeneity probably served the long-range cause of free expression. The diverse society which emerged from the war, despite its attempts to reassert Babbitt-like values, had outgrown its shell. There was more room for diversity in the new one.

There are some critical periods for which knowledge of press freedom is almost totally lacking. The Reconstruction Era is a case in point. Many local editors may have suffered under the yoke of military censorship, but their stories have not been brought to light. Considering how outspoken the Copperhead editors were throughout the Civil War, it is unlikely that they all became mute

[4]For the Spanish-American War, see Charles H. Brown, *The Correspondents' War* (New York, 1967). For World War I, see Zechariah Chafee, Jr., *Free Speech in the United States* (Cambridge, Mass., 1941); Donald Johnson, *The Challenge to American Freedoms* (Lexington, Ky., 1963); H. C. Peterson and Gilbert C. Fite, *Opponents of War 1917–1918* (Madison, Wisc., 1957); Harry N. Scheiber, *The Wilson Administration and Civil Liberties 1917–1921* (Ithaca, N. Y., 1960). Best book on Japanese Evacuation in World War II is Jacobas tenBroek et al., *Prejudice, War and the Constitution* (Berkeley, Calif., 1954). See also Don R. Pember, "The Smith Act as a Restraint on the Press," *Journalism Monograph* 10 (1969).

[5]John P. Roche, *The Quest for the Dream* (New York, 1963), pp. 38–40.

when the military governors took over the states of the Old South. Editors probably were more annoying to some radical governments than to others, but little has been written about them or their effects, if any, in ending these governments, all of which were gone by 1877. Similarly, the many black newspapers which sprang up then have not been discussed in terms either of their influence or the pressures upon them.

Tolerance for dissent can be discussed by topics, such as immigration and the size of towns, as well as by period. Nathan Glazer asserts that the heterogeneity of the seventeenth-century colonies was overcome by the largely homogeneous immigration from the British Isles in the eighteenth century. By the end of that century, 90 percent of the population was of English, Scottish, and Irish extraction. When de Tocqueville toured the U.S. in the 1830s, he saw it not as a patchwork of subcultures but as a land of British origins, modified only slightly by New World conditions. It was the 1840s before immigration accounted for even one-fourth of the American population increase, but the immigrants now came from other areas and destroyed the homogeneity created by the eighteenth-century waves. In the resulting fractionalized society, writers could no longer hope to reach everyone, except at the broadest, platitudinous level of discourse.[6]

Roche believes that the size and nature of the town is a major factor in the growth of urban anonymity which he considers the basis for modern freedom. He says the small town is the seat of reaction. Where everyone knows everyone else's business, there is no place to hide. You either must conform or move to a more congenial place.[7]

The original American colonies were small towns, where residents shared certain central beliefs, usually religious. There was no tolerance for dissenters; even to seek toleration made the seeker a dissenter, and he too had to look for a new home. On one level, there was great freedom of religion in the colonies in that there was a colony for almost every faith. But you had to go to it; you could not expect to advocate "heresy" in an unfriendly locale. Freedom of religion and expression are so intertwined—at least until the

[6]Nathan Glazer, "The Immigrant Groups and American Culture," *Yale Review* 48 (Spring 1959), 382–397.

[7]John P. Roche, *Shadow and Substance* (New York, 1964), pp. 39–47.

time of the American Revolution—that their histories cannot be separated. If religious controversies have stirred us less in the twentieth century—and remember the Darwin fracas of the 1920s—perhaps it is because religion has been less central to our lives. To see what any society really values, see what it shields from criticism.

David Riesman and other writers on the conformity of modern society consider the mass media as contributors to conformity, and certainly the media have helped to standardize tastes and to focus attention on certain ideas and questions. But they have done some things for the nonconformist, too. Today, the village Marxist or nudist can at least subscribe to half a dozen magazines which assure him that somewhere there are other people who share his views. Or he can write letters to the editor of his local paper, who will probably print at least a few. He can find printed reinforcement for every legal system of belief and action, as well as for most of the illegal ones. Never before have the resources for diversity been so rich and varied, a fact often overlooked in talk about the effects of the "mass media," particularly of the massest of them all, network television.

Modern freedom, spawned out of the mutual need for toleration enforced by urban living, is a much more positive type of freedom than the old one which was based on elbowroom. It was easy to be tolerant of a neighbor if his farm was 15 miles away and over a mountain; it is not so easy to be tolerant of him if the eaves of your houses almost touch, if his dog howls at night and keeps you awake, or if his children tromp down your flower beds.

The space analogy applies to the freedom of newspapers. The nineteenth-century frontier press was anything but "free." The printer, often an itinerant who changed loyalties more often than his underwear, simply was hired by the promoters of a fledgling queen city as a publicity agent. His job was to print the "good side" of the town in an effort to attract settlers, businesses, and most important, railroad lines. He printed few, if any, unfavorable local news items, sometimes rationalizing that everybody in the village already knew about shootings or lynchings anyway. When a dream city faded, he simply moved on and gushed as enthusiastically about the next. Such an editor was a kept man, fearful he would lose his happy home, both literally and figuratively.

His role was similar to that of printers like Zenger a century earlier. After all, Zenger was a kind of frontier printer, too—one of only two printers in New York City. More studies comparing frontier printers, both in the United States and in other nations, would go far toward suggesting meaningful generalizations about the role of the press under certain conditions.

Communications history, like all history, would be enriched by more comparative studies, which cross time and/or national boundaries. The major problem with time is technological change; as Einstein remarked that the first atomic explosion changed everything but man's way of thinking, so have other major technological developments dislocated the entire landscape of history. The other type of comparison—between and among contemporary societies—is not so difficult.

Such analyses can enlighten murky corners of our knowledge about the residual effects of certain historical experiences and heritages on freedom of expression. For nearly three-fifths of the time since Columbus's discovery of the New World, this hemisphere was in the grips of the colonial system of European power. British traditions and institutions were quite different from the Spanish, French, and Portuguese, and the history of the colonies was quite different, too. Of course there were also vital differences in geography, climate, and natural resources. Press freedom has fared better in the former British areas, not only of the Western Hemisphere, but in Africa and Asia as well. Why?

Few histories, and no communications histories, have compared the American and Canadian experiences. Both nations had a western wilderness to settle and populate, and presumably the press played a role in Canada as it did in this country. Such reform movements as populism and progressivism had milder manifestations north of the border. Americans sometimes forget about Canada; perhaps because she is so quiet. Canada is fascinating not only as a parallel with American history but also because she has permitted two cultures and two legal traditions to coexist to this day, one French and one English.

No scholar has studied adequately the effects on free expression—both positive and negative—of communications systems and of a common language. A babel of tongues, such as plagues India and much of Africa, prevents citizens from thinking in national terms. It localizes allegiances to tribes or regions, which become in truth the functioning level of society. And at that level there is little toleration for dissent. A nation with a single language is easier to govern, obviously, but it also is a more fertile ground for conspirators.

Communication patterns affected American history drastically. While there was some intercourse within New England colonies, there was virtually none between New England and the southern colonies. It was faster and easier to communicate between Boston and London than between Boston and Georgia, just as it is easier today to place a phone call or send a letter between Lima and London than between Lima and Montevideo.

Some editors still see their primary role as boosters for the home town (and sometimes their vision extends only to the downtown area of it), but there are others who do not hesitate to criticize. Do newspapers in the few cities which still have direct competition do this more than those in cities where the newspapers are under a single ownership? No one has done the research to find out.

Some specialized newspapers and magazines are surprisingly outspoken in their criticisms of the industries they serve. Unfortunately, neither *Editor & Publisher* nor *Broadcasting*, the trade journals of the print and electronic media, fall into this category; they are champions of the richest, fattest ownership elements in their industry. On the other hand, the *Wall Street Journal* has been highly critical of many industries (including the press and radio-television) and has had to weather many an advertising boycott resulting from its exposés.

Another "new look" in American journalism during the 1960s was the new breed of "city magazines," a term which once applied to Chamber of Commerce newsletters designed to attract visitors, conventions, and industry. Now it refers to the new sophisticated crop of big-city magazines which often are more outspoken than the daily newspapers in the same cities.

Any scholar who uses freedom and restraint as his framework should recognize that toleration is an unnatural state. Both men and societies usually opt for short-term goals. Civil liberties require the majority to restrain itself and to permit threats to its dominant position, which is asking a lot. It is "illogical," a situation which becomes understandable, if not logical, when one remembers that an outstanding development of this century has been the rise of civil-liberty elites, drawn from the very sector of society which has most to lose—the rich and powerful. This probably cannot take place in any but highly developed nations.

Seymour Lipset, among others, has pointed out that the lower classes have been anything but a bulwark for enlightened liberalism. In all nations, he found the heaviest ethnic prejudices, rampant nationalism, and communism in the lower classes. Lipset insisted that "Few groups in history have ever voluntarily espoused civil liberties and freedom for those who advocate measures they consider despicable or dangerous."[8] Even Norman Thomas in his old age admitted that he had bet on the wrong horse in his socialist reliance on the lower classes to bring about tolerance. The working class is simply less willing to sacrifice immediate goals for long-term ones; one can argue that they are also less able.

The man who challenges the aims of a nation at war is asking for trouble. Generally he is a man without much power or position who lacks friends with clout. The institutions he might turn to for support are not likely to be very helpful.

Certainly the church is not supportive of this type of dissent. During the Revolution, the clergy were among the principal baiters of Tories, and mobs took care of the few ministers who dared express sympathy. Northern ministers openly attacked Copperhead editors during the Civil War. In the years preceding World Wars I and II, churchmen and intellectuals passed peace resolutions almost to the day of our entry into the war; then their support for the war effort became virtually unanimous.

The universities never have run against public opinion during times of crisis. During World War I they cheerfully cut back or eliminated German language instruction and dismissed faculty members who refused to help lead cheers for the war. During World War II and since, the campuses have served as think-tanks for projects sponsored by the military-industrial complex and have provided expertise for government projects at all levels.

The record of the courts is not much better. Jeffersonians placed much faith in juries to temper prosecutions for sedition, but juries seldom have done so. Perhaps it is unreasonable to expect them to; by definition, jurymen are to represent public opinion, so if that opinion is aflame theirs presumably will be, too. Judges have been no

[8]Seymour Lipset, *Political Man* (New York, 1959), pp. 119–130.

better, even those on the federal bench who are as removed from direct political pressure as any men can be. Again World War I offers a prime example of federal judges handing out maximum 20-year sentences to those convicted of rather trivial violations of the Espionage Act. Even appellate courts upheld those verdicts as they did those contempt of Congress convictions for witnesses who sought protection on First (as opposed to Fifth) Amendment grounds in the "Fearful Fifties."

It would be reassuring to report that the press has been the champion of such friendless dissenters, but it has not. American publishers have always been willing to allow suppression of the radical press; often they have led the efforts to punish it. Many local papers in 1969 were urging and applauding convictions of college and underground editors for printing "dirty words." The general press seldom has been willing to align itself with those elements whose views are unpopular. True, Republican newspapers do not cry out for the wholesale suppression of Democratic papers, but they both cried out at one time for suppression of socialist, communist, and, more recently, underground papers.

Lucy M. Salmon, in *The Newspaper and Authority,* concluded:

> When the liberal and the radical elements of the press have been in disfavor with authority in any form, it has been the press collectively that has been most intolerant of those members of the fraternity with whose views it has not sympathized. In so doing it has been blind to the great principle that it has thereby so much more firmly riveted the shackles of authority on itself. It has confused its personal dislike of the bad taste so often displayed by some of the representatives of this press, its narrow point of view, its self-consciousness, its love of martyrdom, its affection, with the principle of its inalienable right to be all of these things until it learns a more desirable way.[9]

The counsel for the Magazine Publishers Association displayed the same sort of snobbery by applauding the Supreme Court's action in upholding the obscenity conviction of *Eros* on the grounds that respectable publishers never would violate such ground rules anyway. Even such attorneys sometimes forget that the only way to preserve their own freedom is to preserve it for those they hate.

[9]Lucy Salmon, *The Newspaper and Authority* (New York, 1923), p. 460.

During a crisis, real or imagined, those who are trying to hold together a shaky or frightened coalition are not going to permit serious dissent. The cavalry sergeant is simply not going to take a vote on where to set up the circle when the Indians are attacking at full gallop.

> PROPOSITION IV. *The more developed a society, the more subtle will be the controls it exerts on expression.*

Every nation today pays lip service to the concept of free expression. Everyone is for it—if he can define it. A state which assumes its king is infallible obviously cannot tolerate dissent from his views, since the king and the state are one and if he is always right (by definition), then dissent is obviously wrong and not only antiking but antistate. But while there are few unlimited monarchies today, neither are there likely to be any purely libertarian societies in this imperfect world.

The numerous attempts to measure the degree of freedom in various nations have told us largely what we already knew, but they indicate that more developed nations permit more freedom, or at least that those vastly underdeveloped do *not* permit freedom. A certain minimum level of stability is required before a society can worry about such sophisticated concepts as free expression.

Professor Robert Bishop of the University of Michigan, after a survey of world press freedom, concluded that the moving force is economic, allowing for numerous historic accidents. He says that practically no country with a per capita income of less than $600 has democracy because the level of education is too low for people to be effective in the government and because their participation is not needed in a subindustrial society. As the country industrializes, it has to educate its workers, and as they gain education and affluence, they have the need and capacity to participate in politics; as they participate, they gain political power, etc. He finds many restrictions between $600 and $1000 annual per capita income, but essentially a political press. Over $1000 he says there usually is a commercial press with few legal restrictions on it.[10]

[10]Robert Bishop, "Modernization and the European Press" (Paper presented to the Association for Education in Journalism, 1968).

Looking at the restrictions as they appear in a statute book can be misleading, since the spirit of enforcement is not spelled out there. Take, for example, the Espionage Act. More than 2000 Americans were prosecuted under it during World War I, but during World War II there was only one prosecution. It has been in effect since the Presidential proclamation of the Korean emergency in 1950, but its repressive features have not been used to silence dissenters. On the other hand, comparatively innocuous laws, such as local vagrancy or trespass ordinances, often are used effectively to interfere with freedom of expression.

For a visitor from another planet to try to understand our society from reading our constitutions and laws would be almost as misleading as his attempting to do the same from monitoring our network television fare.

The number of laws is not a good indication of the freedom which citizens enjoy, either. Some tribes function with no laws, but their mores and taboos are quite elaborate; indeed, they may be more effective than written laws. Great Britain and the United States have relatively few laws, since they rely on common law and sociological jurisprudence; on the other hand, France has literally thousands of volumes of detailed laws, all curtailing freedom of someone in some way. Does this mean that Frenchmen are "less free" than Britishers or Americans? Of course not, since the French make a game of getting around minor laws as if they did not exist—which, for practical purposes, they do not.

Such a heritage is in itself either a restraint or a protection of a freedom. For example, no American President can eliminate direct contacts with the press, although there is no law requiring press conferences. Either house of Congress can close its doors, but can you imagine the furor if it tried? Judges can bar the press from any courtroom, but few are likely to do so. Most are reluctant to incite the wrath of the press even to the extent of enforcing the relatively modest proposals of the Reardon Report to limit out-of-court statements by attorneys and court officials.

One of the major domestic debates during the quasi-war with France (1798–1800) was whether the United States had inherited the English common law. Jeffersonians argued we had not; Federalists argued that we had. In 1812, there was a clear decision that we had not inherited the English common law of crimes, but certainly much of that tradition was incorporated into our laws and court decisions, and other parts of American law adopted English common law almost undigested. Any decision that would have been *more* restrictive than the English precedent certainly would have been stoutly opposed, even by arch-Federalists. From the first stirrings for freedom, colonists assumed they had the rights of Englishmen; the fuss was over *how much more* freedom they deserved.

As settlers moved West, they never wanted less freedom than they had left behind; that freedom was always used as a starting point for calculating their new liberties. But the society on those frontiers was less developed, less sophisticated. Controls on the press were less subtle. In the established land "back East" (even if that meant one state to the east), as towns developed, the merchants subsidized the press. If the editors got out of line, they might withdraw their advertising or see to it that he lost his printing contracts. On the frontier, the controls were likely to be even more direct—such as wrecking a shop, horse-whipping an editor, or challenging him to a gun duel.[11]

This essay now will consider various kinds of controls, beginning with the most overt and moving to the most subtle; but before that listing is made, the reader should understand the important difference between control exerted before publication and that imposed after publication.

While it might seem that there is little difference when controls are exerted on the press, prior censorship involves a censor who must consider each work before its release. He does not have the option of winking at a work; he must approve or not approve it. If he approves it, it means that the government agrees with the content of the work, and makes subsequent prosecution obviously awkward. On the other hand, a public prosecutor can ignore the material until and unless there is a public clamor for repression. Such selective enforcement may be less predictable but it usually is more permissive. If material is suppressed before it sees the light of day, then obviously it cannot contribute to the public dialogue, a dialogue which is central to the concept of democracy. Even the wildest ideas need

[11]Any student of press freedom will be indebted to Ralph E. McCoy for his monumental bibliographical compilation, *Freedom of the Press* (Carbondale, Ill., 1968). He annotates some 8000 books, pamphlets, articles, and audio-visual materials.

airing, so our theory goes, because today's heresy may well become tomorrow's orthodoxy.

Reliance on post rather than prior restraints also implies more faith by the powers-that-be on the rationality of the citizenry. If we are not quite so naive as John Stuart Mill in our reliance on the good arising out of the free marketplace of ideas, an advanced society does put more faith in the ability of its citizens to discriminate. This faith shows itself in the type of restraints placed on obscenity as well as on political ideas. Modern psychology could build a good case for the proposition that obscenity is in the eye of the beholder. (With the right frame of mind a man can get quite aroused by a mail-order catalog or abstract ink blots.) If that is true, then there can be, by definition, no obscenity (or taboos of whatever kind on written or spoken materials) until they have been beheld.

Supreme Court decisions have been especially critical of prior restraints because of the danger of preventing useful ideas from reaching the public arena and the opportunity for discrimination in enforcement. But aren't such controls as immediate and certain arrest effective and likely to provoke the most common form of prior restraint, restraint at the source? The Court has invalidated legislation which it considered too broad, regardless of its prior or subsequent punishment provision.

Societies do not protect all facets of their media system equally from intrusions on freedom; certainly the United States does not. Here, as throughout most of the world, political speech and writing is the most protected, particularly that which appears in newspapers, and film is the least protected. This correlates with the order in which the Supreme Court "incorporated" these forms into the First Amendment's protective folds by way of the Fourteenth Amendment: speech (1925), newspapers (1931), pamphlets (1934), broadcast (in a series of decisions in the late '30s and early '40s), and finally film in 1951.

GOVERNMENT OWNERSHIP

Outright ownership of the media by the government is the least subtle form of control, but it is the prevailing system in much of the world. In many African nations, the independent newspapers

which sprang to life following independence have either died or
have been seized by the government.

Government ownership of broadcasting systems is even more
common; in fact, the United States is almost alone in relying primarily on private networks. Even the United States was moving
modestly toward limited federal funding for public broadcasting as
the decade of the 1960s ended. State governments, through public
universities, have been in the broadcasting business from its beginnings. New York City has owned its own station for many years.

LICENSING

Next to outright government ownership, the most overt form of control of the mass media is licensing, a procedure subject to discrimination and abuse. While American courts repeatedly have refused
to call film-licensing boards unconstitutional (even the much ad-
judicated Chicago board which is composed exclusively of widows
of policemen), they have made it virtually impossible for such
boards to draw up procedures which the courts will accept. In 1968,
the Supreme Court hinted that it would smile on a tightly drawn
law which established age classification for films and literature
sales, a smile which did not go unnoticed either by the film industry,
which immediately established such a "voluntary" grading of its
films, or by local councilmen and legislators, who set about framing
laws prohibiting sale of "smutty" books and magazines to juveniles.
The rush by the film industry to police itself is symptomatic of the
indirect controls which government agencies can exert in an advanced nation; in a more primitive one, the government simply acts
on its own.

American courts have put tight restraints on municipal and state
licensing of parades, pickets, meetings in public auditoriums, and on
film showings; still the concept of licensing has not been rejected
nor does it appear likely that it will be. Instead, the courts have
moved to reduce the discrimination which issuing officials can use
in handing out the permits. Certainly licensing is not dead at a
federal level in regard to broadcasting.

The federal government began regulating broadcasting only after
the stations pleaded with them to serve as a mechanical traffic cop
to end the wavelength jumping and babel of the airwaves. With

the Federal Radio Act of 1927 and the Federal Communications Act of 1934, the government assumed general supervision over patterns of program content. In truth, it seldom has exercised the option not to renew licenses, but the power is there. Someday it might be used vigorously. What sorts of societal pressures would force such a change in policy?

Is it licensing to select those reporters who will represent the others in "pooling" arrangements at conventions or trials? Certainly it is to a degree. While the media seldom have complained about discrimination on political grounds, this is a potential source of trouble. If such power is exercised for more than crowd control, then it becomes potentially a repressive tool.

SEDITION AND SEDITIOUS LIBEL

Harry Kalven of the University of Chicago Law School, a respected contemporary student of civil liberties, insists in the introduction to *The Negro and the First Amendment* (1965) that the absence of seditious libel as a crime is the "true pragmatic test of freedom of speech" since politically relevant speech is what freedom of speech is all about. He says that any society which has a crime of seditious libel, regardless of its other features, is not a free society.

The more sophisticated a society becomes, the less likely it is to use such blatant weapons as seditious libel against "normal" or "general" publications; but it may shift its fire to publications which advocate unpopular minority positions. During World War I, the Hearst papers went undisciplined by the government for remarks almost identical with those for which socialist and peace-group organs were barred from the mails or prosecuted in courts.

How can we account for the drastic reduction in prosecutions and convictions during World War II? Surely not by the changes in the laws. True, the 1917 Espionage Act had been stripped of its 1918 amendments (which in practice made little difference even in World War I), but otherwise the law still was in effect. Actions under the Espionage Act in World War II were few, and of this handful only one went to the Supreme Court. That one was dismissed for lack of evidence without considering its First Amendment questions, as was the only draft-act case to be reviewed.

The Smith Act had been added to the government's arsenal, but there was only one wartime prosecution for sedition under it. The only state sedition-law case which the Court reviewed was unanimously reversed. Two Jehovah's Witnesses were accused of violating Mississippi's sedition law for distributing literature which criticized the President for sending soldiers overseas to fight, exactly the kinds of sentiments which convicted hundreds, perhaps thousands, of defendants in World War I.

The Espionage Act has been in force since 1950 when President Truman declared a state of emergency in connection with the Korean conflict. In 1953, Congress ruled that the emergency (and its attendant laws including the Espionage Act) would be in force until six months after the President declared the emergency past. No President has ever made this declaration.

So the Espionage Act, the Smith Act, and the draft act all are available to punish Vietnam protestors; still they are not used, although other more specific laws such as those against burning draft cards or mutilating flags are.

Thomas I. Emerson goes so far as to assert that "it is now completely clear that general opposition to the war or defense effort, no matter how vigorously asserted, is constitutionally protected," even if the words might reach men in uniform or might indirectly interfere with the draft system.[12]

LIBEL

Some criminal libel prosecutions, those brought against individuals for spoken or published criticisms of elected public officials, are for all practical purposes seditious libel prosecutions. The decision in *Garrison* v. *Louisiana* (379 U.S. 46) apparently plugged this loophole, but in the half century preceding that case, more than one-fifth of all criminal libel cases which were taken to appellate courts were based on such criticism of officials. Criminal libel is an ancient bugaboo of newsmen, but it is one which has been in decline since the beginning of this century, and with *Garrison* almost, but not quite, disappeared. Most prosecutors tell complainants to use the civil-libel remedy instead.

[12]Thomas I. Emerson, "Freedom of Expression in Wartime," *University of Pennsylvania Law Review* 116 (April 1968), 975–987.

CONTEMPT

Similarly, contempt of court prosecutions have declined sharply in this century. The Supreme Court, in overturning the conviction of California newspapers for contempt in 1941, said in *Bridges* v. *California* (314 U.S. 252) that judges were supposed to have thick skins and should tolerate virtually any press criticisms. It has not upheld a constructive (out-of-court) contempt conviction since. Every few months, some overzealous local judge holds a newsman in contempt, but those cases which are appealed are almost always overturned. There has been revived interest in the use of the contempt power against publications, resulting from the debate over free press and fair trial, but this remained largely talk.

SUBSIDIES

Governments can use the carrot instead of the stick to coerce the media. Subsidies can come in many forms: tax breaks, printing contracts, antitrust exemptions, and low-cost mailing rates. Local, state, and federal governments still grant all these favors to publishers and broadcasters.

Most colonial publishers were postmasters; in addition, they relied on government contracts to print laws, legislative and court proceedings, and public documents. Many nineteenth-century frontier editors, likewise, were postmasters, and most of them existed primarily on the profits from printing legal advertising, particularly in regard to homestead claims.

In spite of the 1945 decision which forced the Associated Press to sell its services to all bonafide applicants (*Associated Press* v. *United States* 326 U.S. 1), newspapers still received many favorable antitrust considerations, such as defining carriers as private contractors instead of employees and allowing joint printing and advertising operations by newspapers in the same community. Newspaper feature syndicates still sell their wares on the basis of territorial exclusivity.

The most pervasive subsidy during the twentieth century has been the postal service. Historians have not given postal subsidies the attention they deserve, although the second-class mailing privilege certainly is a subsidy, an acknowledged one, for the purpose of supporting the dissemination of useful information.

As E. P. Deutsch pointed out 30 years ago, "The newspaper taxes in England were based on the free use, by the taxed newspapers, of the English mails. This free use was carried over into America without the taxes, and then perpetuated, in effect, in the second-class mailing privilege. The privilege is supported here by taxation of all the people, and is justified by the interest of all the people in the unfettered press."[13]

Although the Post Office has never been adequately studied as a repressive force, still it seems clear that no other agency has done so much censoring, both political and moral. Such studies are difficult because the controversies usually are settled in conferences and by written or unwritten orders rather than in courts of law. On an entirely different level, we need to study the effect of the Post Office efficiency, quite aside from its deliberate censorship. George Washington complained that few of his periodicals reached his retirement home at Mount Vernon. They either were late or tattered or stolen from the mails. Such complaints have continued to the present. How reliant have periodicals been on the Post Office at different periods? It is next to impossible to calculate the rates for various classes of mail at various periods, let alone judge the Post Office's effectiveness. One reason the Post Office needs attention from historians is that it has received virtually none from the courts. From 1878 to 1921, no court overruled the department on uses or classes of the mails, and few have done so since.

OBSCENITY

When was the last time that an American newspaper or magazine of general circulation was prosecuted for obscenity? None has had serious difficulties with Post Office censorship since *Esquire* in 1938 (327 U.S. 146). *Eros* hardly qualifies as a general magazine, and the fact that Ralph Ginzburg's prosecution was not brought by the postal authorities indicates how much the censorship scene had shifted in those 30 years since *Esquire*.

On the other hand, publications which lack powerful friends still are prosecuted for obscenity, mostly under state and local laws.

[13]E. P. Deutsch, "Freedom of the Press and of the Mails," *Michigan Law Review* 36 (March 1938), 703–751.

As the decade of the 1960s ended, states were rushing to enact laws patterned after the New York statute upheld by the Supreme Court in *Ginsberg* v. *New York* (390 U.S. 629). This decision established the legality of the "variable obscenity" concept which permits classification of publications or films as objectionable for minors.

Many cities clamped down on distribution of underground papers for use of "naughty" words and pictures. In spite of the new freedom in the theater, performances of shows involving nudity were still being prosecuted in many communities. Some still tried to ban books.

Controls on obscenity lessen as a society matures; partly, but only partly, because the church has less direct control in more sophisticated societies, and obscenity is after all an extension—at least by logic—of blasphemy. A Greek king once eliminated the crime of blasphemy, suggesting that if the gods were offended they should take care of the punishment themselves; modern courts in all but theocracies have said the same to the churches. Certainly as a society matures it narrows the range of punishable words. In the United States today the only taboo words deal with sex and excretion, and those may not stand up much longer. The courts react to changes in mores, and so do the media. This was brought into sharp relief in 1969 when the Associated Press transmitted the text of the Walker Commission report on the Chicago disorders which included words which editors traditionally replaced with asterisks or blanks. Some editors did; others let the text run; all agreed it was a borderline case.

ACCESS

Openness in government is a characteristic of more advanced, sophisticated societies. The United States, almost alone, has adopted open-meeting and open-record laws plus laws which permit reporters to refuse to tell courts or grand juries their sources of information; however, only 14 states have such "shield laws," and courts seldom have upheld a common law right to withhold such information. Other Western democracies have not felt the need for such laws, and many American editors say such laws do more harm than good because once the inevitable exceptions are written down, legal eagles who are members of boards and commissions will spot a reason why that meeting or record falls in such a category. The real effects of such laws is a topic which cries for attention, particularly in light of the related problems raised by the subpoenaeing of reporters, notes and TV footage.

In spite of such laws, the openness of American government is by no means absolute. Nearly half of congressional committee meetings are held in secret, cameras and broadcasting equipment are barred from most courtrooms and the floors of Congress, and, perhaps most important, there is a natural reluctance of lower-rung bureaucrats to reveal anything which might put them or their bosses in a bad light. The sometimes bitter wrangle over the free press-fair trial issue suggested many questions worthy of research in this area.

SELF-IMPOSED RESTRAINTS

I. F. Stone, the publisher of a newsletter which regularly strikes out at American journalism as well as other social manifestations, says that controls on the American press are more subtle than they once were, but that they are nonetheless effective.

> In the first place, the average publisher is not a newspaperman; he's somebody who happened to make his money in some other business; very often he'd like a tax-loss for his income tax; he picks up his ideas in the locker-room of the local country club, and he doesn't know very much; people who have spent all their life in the business have to kowtow to his prejudices. The important thing about the so-called communications industry in America is that it's basically concerned with merchandising. News is a kind of by-product. And if you want to sell things, you don't want to offend anybody. There is a tendency toward blandness.[14]

Are those assertions about publishers and their motives true? We don't have enough hard data to know about today's publishers, let alone yesterday's. Much of the necessary data is still lodged in government records and local histories. Do many publishers use their properties as tax losses, and if so does it make any difference

[14]I. F. Stone, "Late Night Line Up," *The Listener* 80 (October 31, 1968), 582.

in their products? Is the content of profitable papers different from that of unprofitable ones?

Although publishers are fond of saying their product has to be "reelected" every day by its subscribers, this makes little sense in our overwhelmingly monopolistic press situation. A related question is whether it makes any sense even in a competitive situation. There is a whole realm of research needed on the effects of competition on the press.

Communications researchers have suggested sensationalism indices to measure press content; perhaps they need a blandness index. It might—or might not—correlate with large circulation.

In some ways such economic controls—controls of the marketplace, if you will—are the most subtle, and the most effective of all.

•   •   •

Those in power are likely to overestimate the power of the spoken or written word. They overestimate its positive effects as a propaganda device, and they overestimate even more its negative effects as a threat. Even the buzzing of a fly can sound like a termite to a man seated on a wooden throne.

When society feels threatened it grows impatient with whatever brand of radicalism is most visible. Southern states in the 1830s and 1840s imposed heavy penalties for distribution or possession of antislavery literature, disregarding the fact that few slaves could read. During World War I, the favorite targets of legal and extralegal suppression also were economic heretics: socialists, Industrial Workers of the World, and the Non-Partisan League. The cloak of patriotism, then as now, served the majority who were bent on teaching the upstarts a lesson. In the 1960s, impatience with dissent was focused on the twin revolutions of the blacks and youth. The fights over four-letter words in underground and campus papers were but public manifestations of society's growing impatience with radicalism.

If society always reacts in this way, then it would tend to confirm Siebert's propositions. Perhaps the questions raised in this essay will stimulate further testing and analysis of them. One conclusion is very clear: We need more research about free expression and less rhetoric.

3 POLITICS, ECONOMICS, AND THE MASS MEDIA

William E. Ames and Dwight L. Teeter

William E. Ames, University of Washington, is a former president of the Association for Education in Journalism and head of its History Division, as well as the author of many articles and papers. *Dwight L. Teeter,* University of Wisconsin, is coauthor of *Law of Mass Communications* and contributor of chapters to two other books.

It is no doubt significant that more is known about the love life of many a prominent publisher than is known about the financial lives of their newspapers. But then, perhaps sex is more fun for historians than is money. The cynic might argue that publishers (or other media entrepreneurs) are most reticent about what matters most to them. So, figures on boudoir sheets may be guessed at (if not known for sure); figures on balance sheets somehow remain a murkier mystery.

To understand the media,[1] to see them more nearly whole in historical terms, means that the economic dimension must no longer be neglected. Historians are aware of such neglect: For example, a 1968 survey of journalism history teachers indicated that "economics of the press" is the historical topic which most desperately needs more work. A related topic, "labor and the press," was named almost as often as an area needing study.[2]

This essay, inelegantly devoid of theory, models, and other esoterica of the social sciences, is a call for good descriptive studies of the political-economic lives of units of the mass media and of the persons who control those units. Very little of this description has been done. Information needed to give meaningful interpretation to the political and economic roles which the press in the United States has played simply has not been collected and presented by historians. Without such information, it is difficult to put the political functioning of the press of almost any period into proper perspective.

Once more is known, then perhaps it will be time to apply some of the more sophisticated tools of economic analysis to communications history. Perhaps the slogan should be: Data First! One hopes, if faintly, that what Abraham Kaplan has called the law of the instrument will not be put to work in this area, at least not for a while. As new research tools come into vogue, they are used gaily, gaily, in situations where such tools are not always helpful. Hence, the law of the instrument: "Give a small boy a hammer and he will find that everything he encounters needs pounding."[3]

After such an invocation, asking new reverence for the study of political-economic aspects of communications history, such an overwhelmingly, defeatingly broad topic, will be set aside. The overriding purpose of this chapter is to suggest some kinds of needed research about the political economics of communications, with special emphasis upon the intersection of private and governmental forces with freedom (and suppression) of expression in the mass media.

The authors of this essay suggest that political-economic study of the media is not only needed but also possible. In so doing, it is not

[1]This phrase is used by special arrangement with Marshall McLuhan.

[2]John D. Stevens and Donald L. Shaw, "Research Needs in Communications History: A Survey of Teachers," *Journalism Quarterly* 45:3 (Autumn 1968), 547–549.

[3]Abraham Kaplan, *The Conduct of Inquiry* (San Francisco, 1964), p. 28.

asserted that such study is the only proper approach to communications history. The perils of monistic theories of causation are too readily apparent; the population explosion, for one thing, suggests that there are factors other than economic which affect the behavior of mankind, or of the communications media.

One trouble with any kind of economic history is that it is commonly perceived as "proving," simultaneously, too little and too much. It proves too little, generally, because the historian almost always has to work with terribly incomplete evidence. And it proves too much because the historian who looks at economic considerations is apt to be tagged with that most pejorative phrase, "economic determinist." Such labels seem to be misapplied—see the manifold misreadings of the late Charles A. Beard's *An Economic Interpretation of the Constitution* (1913)—despite anguished cries from the author that he never claimed that the economic variable was the *only* important consideration.[4]

Unfortunately, it seems that the more a topic needs study, the harder it is to find the necessary source materials. For example, a 1969 survey of some major manuscript holdings indicated that materials bearing on the economic aspects of mass communications history were scarcer than for any other topics.[5] It may be objected that financial data is so hard to come by that exhortations to provide more economic history of the communications media must have a hollow ring. History, it may be said, is the art of the possible, and is possible only where some kind of records survive. And journalists—

[4]For example, two of Beard's critics, Robert Eldon Brown and Forrest McDonald, evidently were dismayed by Beard's suggestion that economic considerations may have played their part when the Founding Fathers wrote the Constitution. Beard, indeed, had declared that the Constitution was the work of a "consolidated group." Both Brown and McDonald, however, inaccurately paraphrased Beard's conclusion to read that the Constitution was "the work of consolidated *economic* groups." The addition of the italicized word suggests that historians Brown and McDonald were overly eager to set right what they considered to be the errors of one dead political scientist: Charles Austin Beard. See Brown, *Charles A. Beard: A Critical Analysis of "An Economic Interpretation of the Constitution"* (Princeton, N. J., 1956), p. 20; McDonald, *We The People: The Economic Origins of the Constitution* (Chicago, 1958), p. vii.

[5]Unpublished Report of the Association for Education in Journalism, History Division Bibliography Committee for 1968–1969.

reporters, editors, publishers, broadcasters—are notoriously reluctant to save personal or financial materials about themselves. Attempts are now being made—as at the Mass Communications History Center of the State Historical Society of Wisconsin—to save personal and business papers of influential communicators.

If personal documents and records of journalists are rare, financial records of media men and institutions are virtually impossible to locate. And once historians locate them, they may well find other problems, as the late Professor Howard K. Beale suggested in a discussion of the pitfalls of business history:

> Business history presents a particularly difficult problem. Business records, until recently, have been so rarely available that when they are opened there is a special feeling of gratitude. Or they are furnished as a favor to a particular author. Everybody is nervous lest, if business is offended by business history, further records will not be made available. Authors who use them often have to agree to restriction and supervision to get them at all. One competent scholar was told by the director of a repository that has research funds that he might be considered for a grant for study of business history if he would change his views. Sometimes the business whose history is being written has paid handsomely in expense money if not more directly. Some business historians are attracted to the field in the first place because they have a sense of the great contribution business men have made to our life; others enter the field because they feel the wickedness of business should be exposed. Neither motive promises well for sound history. The saving factor here, along with some middle-of-the-road scholars, is that the historians who do hold these more extreme and opposite points of view watch each other closely and criticize each other with such zest that they probably force each other to moderately sound positions.[6]

If the historians of business have trouble remaining independent of their data-granting benefactors, then what of the press's dependence on its financial supporters? Commentators on the media today fret—sometimes with considerable justification—about the failures of journalists to remain independent of the influences of government

[6]Howard K. Beale, "The Professional Historian: His Theory and Practice," *Pacific Historical Review* 22:3 (August 1953), 227–255.

or business. One of the most devastating slurs which can be directed toward a newsman is to say that he is "in the pocket" of some government agency or of some business. But when this idea is pushed back into the eighteenth or nineteenth centuries, it immediately appears that many printers or publishers, including those whose firms produced newspapers, *wanted* to climb right into government's pocket.

Incidents of active seeking of government printing subsidies are very much a part, if largely untold, of our nation's journalism history. During the War for Independence, for example, printer Robert Aitken and several of his competitors even petitioned Congress for permission to publish an *official* Bible for the United States, and asked for monopoly privileges at home plus an embargo on the importation of Bibles from abroad. Although these printers were ultimately disappointed, a committee of Congress gave close study to their proposition.[7] Such scrambles for governmental support, which more often included somewhat lesser joustings among publishers for work as "official" or "public" printers of laws, statutes, legislative minutes, and the like, were merely one way in which publishers could bring in revenue. Until well into the nineteenth century, neither advertising revenues nor circulation receipts—nor a combination of the two—was likely to be enough to support a newspaper. Governmental money for public printing was welcome and often downright necessary to survival.

The influence of economic factors on freedom—or restriction—of expression is, of course, older than printing. Power, including government and economic power, seldom likes to be opposed, be it by conversation, broadside, or telecast. In point is the lament voiced by eighteenth-century printer Isaiah Thomas of the *Massachusetts Spy,* a man held by some historians to be among the foremost printers of the American Revolution. Thomas wrote: "One of my profession must be either of one party or the other (he cannot please both) he must therefore incur censure of the opposite party

---

[7]Papers of the Continental Congress, 1774–1789, Microcopy No. 247, National Archives Microfilm Publications (Reel 66, Item 46), Summer 1777; Willman and Carol Spawn, "Robert Aitken, Colonial Printer of Philadelphia," unpaged extract from *Graphic Arts Review,* January–February 1960; Worthington C. Ford et al., eds., *Journals of the Continental Congress, 1774–1789* (Washington, D.C., 1904–1937), vol. 23, pp. 572–574.

. . . though caressed and encouraged by others. . . ."[8] Thomas's words represent the persons who have provided this nation with its newspapers, magazines, motion pictures, and radio and television broadcasts: businessmen who are (or who may be made subject to) political and/or economic pressures.

The graceless "and/or" phrase in the preceding sentence is crucial here. "Political and/or economic pressures. . . ." The authors of this essay acknowledge that politics can be studied alone, so can economics, but where communications history is concerned, it seems to us to make more sense to study economic and political controls or pressures together. For communications history, there seems to be much truth in the notion that economics are the result of politics, and vice versa.

Such an assertion, however, should not be uncritically applied. Paying the piper has not always meant calling the tune where the press is concerned. Individual media units and journalists must be studied. Some servile journalists are quite fully described in a number of studies of the frontier—sometimes called "booster"—press.[9] Earlier, during the American Revolution, printers' active seeking of governmental printing subsidies may be seen in many records of colonial and state governments and in the *Journals of the Continental Congress*. This enthusiastic seeking of government funds, however, did not mean that printers necessarily abstained from printing savage criticisms of the conduct of public affairs. John Dunlap of the *Pennsylvania Packet*, for example, seemed to take an almost perverse delight in using his newspaper to embarass the very same politicians who had helped him to get government printing business.[10] Tame gratitude was not always the reward for economic support.

In an effort to suggest some of the kinds of political and economic studies which may be undertaken, four topical case studies will be presented, drawn in part from the authors' research in

[8]Clifford K. Shipton, *Isaiah Thomas: Printer, Patriot, and Philanthropist* (Rochester, N.Y., 1948), p. 22.

[9]E.g., George S. Hage, *Newspapers on the Minnesota Frontier, 1849–1860* (Minneapolis, Minn., 1967), and Daniel J. Boorstin, *The Americans: The National Experience* (New York, 1965), pp. 124–134.

[10]Dwight L. Teeter, "Press Freedom and the Public Printing: Pennsylvania, 1775–1783," *Journalism Quarterly* 45:3 (Autumn 1968), 445–451.

eighteenth- and nineteenth-century journalism history. Economic history is here seen as being much more than ledgers and balance sheets, which are most often unavailable anyway. Economics includes such matters as circulation patterns and the changing relationships between media and government. These small studies are purposely suggestive rather than exhaustive.

NEWSPAPER CIRCULATION:
THE BRADFORDS' *PENNSYLVANIA JOURNAL*, 1776–1778

Relatively little has been written about newspaper circulation during the early years of the United States. There was, of course, no Audit Bureau of Circulation, and historians, in the absence of other information, have had to make do with publishers' own claims about circulations. As Arthur M. Schlesinger suggested, there is "inherent credibility" in some circulation figures, especially in the general upward trend in the number of subscribers.[11] Lacking "newsstand" or "street" sales of more recent times, annual or semiannual subscriptions were a common method used during the eighteenth century to bring in revenue. With a yearly subscription, half might be taken "in advance" at the time a person agreed to receive a newspaper. The second half of the subscription was then due and payable in six months, although subscribers were evidently very slow in meeting such obligations.[12]

In late colonial times, according to printer-historian Isaiah Thomas, a subscription list of about 600 was needed for a newspaper to make ends meet.[13] And it is known that in 1754, when four competing weekly newspapers were struggling along in Boston, each had about that average weekly circulation.[14]

Beyond figures such as these, however, the historian finds himself in a never-never land made up of the claims of biased witnesses. James Rivington claimed a circulation of 3600 for his Tory *New*

[11]Arthur M. Schlesinger, *Prelude to Independence: The Newspaper War on Great Britain 1764–1776* (New York, 1958), Appendix A, pp. 303–304.

[12]Advertisement in the *Pennsylvania Journal*, January 25, 1775.

[13]Isaiah Thomas, *The History of Printing in America*, rev. ed., 2 vols. (Worcester, Mass., 1874), 2: 8, 17.

[14]Schlesinger, *op. cit.*, p. 303.

York Gazetteer in 1775. The *Boston Gazette* listed its weekly circulation as 2000 in 1775, while Isaiah Thomas's rival *Massachusetts Spy* said that its circulation was 3500.[15]

However interesting such numbers games might be for antiquarians, they are of little importance in any effort to evaluate newspapers of the American Revolution. The tiny newspapers, often running to only four pages, were read for every single word, even though they often contained more advertising than news. These printed sheets were popular diversions in the taverns, coffee houses, shops, and inns where people read newspapers or heard them read aloud. If newspapers were read avidly near their place of publication, they were received with equal interest in other areas, colonies, and provinces. As Merrill Jensen has noted, the printers "made constant use of scissors so that the same news item or political essay often appears in the newspapers all the way from New Hampshire to Georgia, sometimes with acknowledgment and sometimes not."[16]

Although many historians have relied heavily upon newspapers as sources, they have often had difficulty in estimating newspapers' circulations. A respected scholar, Robert M. Brunhouse, has suggested that Pennsylvania's newspapers were important primarily in Philadelphia during the War for Independence. Brunhouse noted that until the middle 1780s, all newspapers were Philadelphia-based. He added that "their circulation in the hinterland was limited and news was stale by the time it reached those parts."[17] News may have been "stale" by our standards by the time it reached hamlets to the west, but it was eagerly sought nonetheless. Brunhouse evidently did not understand newspaper circulation patterns in Pennsylvania during the Revolution. To date, historians—including Brunhouse and the elder Schlesinger—overlooked a seldom-used item in the rich collections of the Historical Society of Pennsylvania: printer William Bradford's "List of Subscribers on the 25th of August 1775 *et postea* to the Pennsylvania Journal." This handwritten circulation ledger shows that the *Journal*'s circulation in Philadelphia in

[15]*Ibid.*, 303–304.

[16]Merrill Jensen, *The New Nation: A History of the Articles of Confederation, 1781–1789* (New York, 1950), p. 430.

[17]Robert M. Brunhouse, *The Counter-Revolution in Pennsylvania, 1776–1790* (Philadelphia, 1942), p. 5.

mid-1775 was small, amounting to only 220 subscribers. There were far more subscribers to the paper in Pennsylvania, but outside of "the city and liberties of Philadelphia." The *Journal* had more than 400 subscribers listed by the Bradfords in 1776. Since the *Journal's* total circulation was roughly 2400 in late 1776, the importance of subscribers in other states is readily apparent.[18]

Although the *Journal's* circulation in Philadelphia seems quite small—220 subscribers in a city of 35,000, then the largest on the North American continent—the Bradford's newspaper reached the rich and powerful men of the city, the heads of the political factions during the late 1770s. These leaders were, by and large, closely tied by business and religious connections, and sometimes by family bonds.[19]

The 1767 Philadelphia circulation list of the *Journal* was a virtual "Who's Who" of the city. Subscribers included William Allen, Tory Chief Justice of colonial Pennsylvania; Robert Morris, then a rising merchant; Benjamin Chew, a wealthy Quaker politician; Joseph Galloway, political boss of the antiproprietary faction; and John Dickinson, leader of the rival group. Also included in the list were a few "new men" such as Daniel Roberdeau, who were to be important in the revolutionary struggle. But by and large, the *Journal's* Philadelphia circulation list in 1767 echoed the names of powerful old families or of men connected to them: Joseph Shippen, Jr., James Biddle, James Benezet, "Dr. Cadwallader," and Thomas Willing.[20]

When Colonel Bradford counted his "town [Philadelphia] subscribers" in February 1776, he added in a leaven of "new men," some of whom played important roles in the Revolution. Listed together were the names of the conservative "Robert Aitkin" [sic] and the radical Thomas Paine, who had recently left the employ of Aitken's printing house. Named also was a group disturbing to conservatives—the "Marine Committee." Also appearing among the 1776 circulation figures for the *Journal* were men who doubtless appeared to be "rabble" to conservative Philadelphians. Bradford's 1776

[18]"Bradford's List of Subscribers," Manuscript Collections, Historical Society of Pennsylvania, Philadelphia.

[19]William S. Hanna, *Benjamin Franklin and Pennsylvania Politics* (Palo Alto, Calif., 1964), pp. 3–4.

[20]"Bradford's List of Subscribers," *op. cit.*

city list included the likes of "Robert Smith sailmaker" in addition
to the mainstays of pre-Revolutionary Pennsylvania such as Thomas
Willing and John Dickinson.

In charting the destinations of more than 2300 copies of the
Pennsylvania Journal, Bradford followed a general pattern. Repro-
duced below is a page of the circulation account book for Burlington, New Jersey.

NUMBER BEGAN AT	1 BURLINGTON	NUMBER LEFT OFF AT
	Josiah F. Davenport Esqr. Post Master	
	The Burlington Stage	
1488	Isaac Collins Esqr. Printer	
	John Inglis	
	John Fenimore	
	~~His Excellency William Franklin~~	
	sent to	a Tory
	~~Charles Pettit~~ Esqr. *Carried to Haddonfield*	
1762	James Craft—Burlington	
1593	John Carles Esqr.	
1594	Alexander Chisholm	

The "number began at" column, although not carried out with
much consistency by Bradford, referred to the number of an issue.
This column allowed the printer to see just when someone had
begun subscribing to the *Journal* so that Bradford could bill him
at the end of six months or a year if the subscriber did not pay
the post rider or the stage driver or the tavern keeper who helped
circulate the *Journal.* Burlington's James Craft, for example, began
his subscription with issue number 1762, which meant that the
first issue received by Craft was that for Wednesday, September 11,
1776.

In the center column, the printer listed persons who received the
Journal. Sometimes, this meant that one name would be listed for
each newspaper sent. Other times, as in listing Haddonfield, New
Jersey, Bradford would note that a bundle of six was to be left
with "Hugh Creighton, Tavern Keeper to whose care the Packet
must be Directed, & to be charged at half Price."

Doing business over long distances when communication was slow and at best uncertain was difficult for printers. One post rider asked Thomas Bradford "to send . . . word by the bearer or Otherwise, as (Soon as possible) *at what rate* the Subscribers to the Neshaminey Packets of News Papers must pay for the half-Year already Commenced." Prospective subscribers also tried to suggest how the *Journal* might be sent to them. One letter from "the forks of Egg Harbour in Gloucester County, Virginia," suggested that the writer had an "opportunity to receive them by Stage. . . ."

The *Journal* and other newspapers of the time were prized by readers up and down the coast. A sarcastically impatient letter from Samuel Freeman of Falmouth, Massachusetts, asked why the *Journal* was so tardy in appearing after he had asked to be added to the list of subscribers. Freeman admitted that his request might not have reached the Bradfords. But he added: "If you did [receive the request] I suppose you deem'd the [Falmouth Post] Office of too little importance to be honour'd with a Philadelphia Paper—& if so—I have no more to say for I cannot plead any thing in favour of it more than my wish to have the earliest News of Public Speculations that comes from your Press— . . . P.S. If you send it only a few weeks while our General Court [legislature] is sitting here, it will be acceptable."[21]

Although much useful information about the Bradfords' dealings with post riders and subscribers may be gleaned from scattered letters, the best picture may be obtained by leafing through the *Journal*'s circulation book, written for the most part in the haphazard scrawl of Colonel William Bradford. Occasional notes were scribbled in the book by his son and partner, Thomas, or by his youngest son (and future attorney-general of Pennsylvania and the United States), William, Jr., who sometimes helped around the printing house. These notations indicate, for example, that Peter Withington's tavern in Reading was a stage and post stop and a major newspaper distribution point for Berks and Cumberland Counties in Pennsylvania. Once newspapers reached Withington's, William Carheart took a bundle of seven newspapers from the tavern to the residence of Tobias Hendricks in Cumberland County.

[21]All three letters in John William Wallace Collection, Historical Society of Pennsylvania, Philadelphia.

Hendricks then distributed the *Journal* to subscribers who lived nearby.

Similarly, bundles of the *Journal* were taken to Delaware, by post rider Thomas Sculley. Sculley left 20 newspapers at Dover and made scattered stops to deliver mail and other newspapers. Eighteen other copies of the *Journal* moved by stage to "Woodberry, by George Johnson [a stage driver], from Hyder's Ferry."

Once out of Pennsylvania, the paths traveled by copies of the *Journal* were many and varied. Papers left at "Captain Lon's" (a captain of a coasting ship) in Philadelphia were destined for "sundrey places." One such place was the printing house of John Hunter Holt, the young man who tried to start business in Norfolk but whose press was stolen by Lord Dunmore's British troops and carried off in a British warship.

Despite all the difficulties inherent in the complicated processes of getting newspapers to subscribers who lived far from Philadelphia, about 90 percent of the *Journal*'s circulation total of roughly 2400 was outside of the city. More important than the mere number of the newspaper's subscribers, however, were the persons reached by the *Journal*. Its circulation during the War of Independence, both in Philadelphia and in outlying areas, included many men who were important political leaders, or important "information disseminators," such as postmasters, tavern keepers, or newspaper publishers. Eight of the Bradfords' newspapers sent to "Connecticutt" in 1776 were addressed to these men: "The Post Master in Hartford, Thomas Green Printer Do. [Ditto] Timothy Green Printer New London, Parker & Company Printers O' New Haven, Silas Deane, Esq'r. [an important merchant and politician], and Alexander & James Robertson Printers, Norwich." Only two copies of the *Journal* went to Westmoreland County, Virginia, but one was addressed to one of the most powerful politicians of the American Revolution, Richard Henry Lee. Circulation patterns which included such political leaders and printers insured maximum impact for newspapers.

The vigorous political dialogues in the Philadelphia newspapers in 1775 and 1776 were important beyond the city and beyond the boundaries of Pennsylvania. Philadelphia printers, and perhaps all American printers of the late eighteenth century, were publishers for a continent. Their newspapers, broadsides, or printed sermons traveled by post-rider saddlebag, by stage, and by sailing ships to all of the thirteen colonies and beyond. Men wrote freely about politics for the Philadelphia newspapers, and their opinions on matters affecting the developing revolution could be read throughout America.

POLITICAL PATRONAGE AND THE PARTY PRESS, 1800–1846

One of the greatest unexplored areas in communications history is the period between the adoption of the Constitution and the start of the Civil War. Many assertions about the political functions and role of the newspapers published during that period have been made, as Charles A. Beard once said in another context, without fear and without research. Conclusions have been drawn without sufficient collection and careful analysis of data. The late Frank Luther Mott, in his widely used text, *American Journalism: A History 1690–1960* (1962), devoted much of his nearly 900 pages to listings of who published what newspapers, when, and where. There was little delving into political, economic, and social implications of the development of the mass media in this country. The political press of the nineteenth century was dismissed under such critical chapter headings as "The Dark Ages of Partisan Journalism." The period following was greeted as "The Development of the News Function." Elsewhere, Mott referred to the role of government patronage with this comment: "A more insidious encroachment on press freedom came by way of state printing contracts and legal publications for government."

Edwin Emery in *The Press in America* (1962) gave many more pages to a discussion of William Randolph Hearst than he did to the entire 70 years when the political press dominated the journalism of the nation. Likewise, Alfred McClung Lee, who relied so heavily on economic patterns in developing his history of the daily newspaper in America, barely mentioned the role of patronage in supporting American newspapers.[22]

No one has yet published a careful study of the newspapers which were strongly tied to the Republic during its formative years

[22]Alfred McClung Lee, *The Daily Newspaper in America* (New York, 1937).

in Philadelphia. Yet, it is known that from the earliest days of the nation, federal printing business provided a financial base which enabled a number of newspapers to remain in existence. Such newspapers were subsidized, in important measure, to provide support for the political philosophies espoused by the editors. Congress early adopted the recommendation that the Secretary of State and the Clerk of the House be authorized to contract with printers to execute necessary printing and binding "on the most reasonable terms." These expenses were met from the contingency fund, each bill being accounted for by a separate voucher. This accounts for the difficulty of researching this period for printing costs, since many of those vouchers are missing.[23]

Before the United States government was moved to Washington, D.C., in 1880, the system was clearly established that the administration in power would use federal patronage to underwrite a program of positive support through the newspapers backing that particular party. Such support, rather than yielding large profits for the printers, usually provided only the margin necessary to keep a newspaper in business. Newspapering, during the early years of the Republic, was rarely lucrative. Editors experienced great difficulty in collecting subscriptions from outside the immediate urban circulation area of the newspaper, and the income from advertisements was, by today's standards, very small. As one colonial editor complained, "Subsisting by a country news-paper, is generally little better than starving. . . ."[24]

Several systems of leasing the printing contracts were used by the federal government during the first half of the nineteenth century, but the one most closely tied to the political facts of the nation passed Congress in 1819. The new system of printing patronage, devised by Senator Henry Clay of Kentucky, halted the practice of awarding contracts to the lowest bidder. Instead, each house of Congress was given the power to choose the firm which it desired to handle the large volume of printing generated by each session. This effectively removed the contracts from the large printing houses which had been built up in the nation's capital and placed the

[23]John H. Powell, *The Books of a New Nation 1774–1814* (Philadelphia, 1957), p. 85.

[24]Quoted in Noble E. Cunningham Jr., *The Jeffersonian Republicans in Power* (Chapel Hill, N.C., 1963), p. 247.

government's printing in the hands of the newspapers. This was clearly part of Clay's plan to woo support from the Washington, D.C., newspapers in his bid for the presidency.[25]

There were other results from Clay's 1819 patronage bill which greatly affected the development and functioning of the capital's political newspapers. The bill enabled each house to select a newspaper spokesman so that the country had congressional as well as Presidential quasi-official journals. This was important, for in the years between 1819 and 1846, these printing contracts enabled newspapers opposing the administration to remain alive and to provide a voice for various splinter factions which developed in the politics of the nation. By the 1830s, during the administration of Andrew Jackson, three of the four newspapers published in Washington opposed the administration and the dominant political party. Despite such opposition, these papers were able to remain in business because of various patronage contracts which included the congressional printing as well as special projects such as the American State Papers, the Annals of Congress, and the American Archives. All were published by Whig editors who opposed the Jackson administration on nearly every major piece of legislation proposed.

But such opposition to the Jackson administration did not mean that newspapers such as the *National Intelligencer* sold their independence to the Whig party in return for its support. The *Intelligencer*'s publishers, Joseph Gales and William Winston Seaton, had at least three printing contracts from the federal government, which helped keep them publishing so they could strenuously oppose the Jackson administration. At the same time, however, Gales and Seaton refused to follow the narrow dictates of the Whig party. No faction of the party was satisfied with the *Intelligencer* editors' refusal to support one of the Whig candidates who sought the nomination in order to oppose Martin Van Buren for the Presidency.

Daniel Webster, a party leader, complained of the independence of the *Intelligencer* in this way: "If Messrs. G. [Gales] and S. [Seaton] are not disposed to support, at present, any named Candidate, they might at least, preach the necessity of supporting *a*

[25]See John Quincy Adams' Diary, July 28, 1822, quoted in *Memoirs of John Quincy Adams* (Philadelphia, 1875), vol. 6, pp. 46–47.

Whig candidate—*some* Whig candidate. We are in danger of breaking up, & dividing. Our national field marshall—he that would rally & encourage us, is the leading paper on our side."[26]

Although the patronage support of the *Intelligencer* continued over the next decade, that newspaper's political independence was not lessened. The climax of the relationship between the *Intelligencer* and the Whig party came in 1849 when a Whig President, Zachary Taylor, bypassed Gales and Seaton's newspaper as he selected the quasi-official spokesman for his administration. As a Taylor adviser saw it, Gales and Seaton had followed far too independent a path for years to be of much service to the party or to the new Whig President. They were "committed to ultra measures." The adviser further contended "[t]hat they [Gales and Seaton] never did find out that Tyler [President John Tyler] was not a good Whig. That they have always taken the foreign side in every dispute the country has been in since the war with England, so much so, that many people suspect them of having been bribed. . . ."[27]

Such descriptions of what was the longest lived and probably the most influential of all the political newspapers in the country hardly says much about journals which were the handmaidens of either the political parties or of the federal government. The *Intelligencer* without doubt received more patronage payments from the federal government than any newspaper in the history of the nation.

Yet despite all the money which the *Intelligencer*'s editors received from the federal government—largely through the support of the Whig party—the newspaper did not become the sycophantic spokesman for its supporters. The patronage printing jobs which the newspaper received, since they were mainly long-term printing contracts, enabled it to maintain a position of greater independence than most American newspapers, before or since.[28]

For all practical purposes, the patronage system which had underwritten (and in a way created) a number of independent

[26]Daniel Webster to Nicholas Biddle, May 12, 1835, Biddle Papers (Library of Congress, Washington, D.C., 64).

[27]A. T. Burnley to John Crittenden, January 12, 1849, Crittenden Papers (Library of Congress, Washington, D.C., vol. 13).

[28]William E. Ames, "Federal Patronage and the Washington, D.C., Press" (Paper presented to the Association for Education in Journalism, 1967).

newspapers ceased to function by 1850. The system died for a number of reasons, some of which were economic. The popular penny press introduced into the country in the early 1830s demonstrated that sensationalism and a cheap price could attract a mass audience and provide a financial base for the press. With mass audiences came mass advertising, and the new source of support encouraged newspaper publishers to break the umbilical cord which tied them to political parties and to government patronage. This new method of support had its advantages; the government patronage system had held many dangers for the individual publisher.

As Washington publisher John C. Rives put it:

> The risk of election, of re-election—the great rapidity, dispatch and punctuality required—the illegibility and imperfection of a great portion of the manuscript sent—the extra wates for work necessarily done at night and on Sunday—the necessity of employing a large number of first-rate journeymen instead of apprentices—and the high per cent of premium demanded for insurance of such establishments—are among the chief considerations of disadvantages which present themselves to those who are acquainted with Congressional printing.[29]

One of the major advantages of the patronage system—one frequently overlooked—was the quantity and quality of the reporting of the congressional debates and proceedings which the patronage-supported newspapers supplied. With less need to attract large audiences with popular reading fare, the publishers of patronage-aided papers could concentrate upon publishing in-depth reports and accounts of the proceedings in Congress and also in other agencies of government. In addition to being newspapers, the Washington press also played the role of the Congressional record of its day. And, to suggest a further advantage, the "patronage newspapers" did not include spurious "speeches" never delivered as today's *Congressional Record*. They did, however, do considerable editing for partisan purposes.[30]

[29]John C. Rives testimony, given in House Report 298, 26th Cong., 1st sess.

[30]Elizabeth Gregory McPherson, "The History of Reporting the Debates and Proceedings of Congress" (Ph.D. diss., University of North Carolina, 1940).

The patronage system meant that each party had at least one newspaper to support its point of view in the nation's capital and to report its political actions to the nation. Until the invention of the telegraph and the advent of the press services, these newspapers provided the extensive coverage of federal government which was copied into other party newspapers across the country. Hiring trained stenographers to take down, transcribe, revise, and correct the debates was a costly process but certainly provided a praise-worthy service for the Washington, as well as the national, political community.

Governmental support of the information system had many positive attributes, perhaps best explained by John C. Rives, copublisher of the *Washington Globe:*

> I recommend it because it keeps up two daily papers here, advocating the principles and interests . . . of the two great parties into which the Union is happily . . . divided; each of them giving full and fair reports of the debates in Congress, which . . . is worth more to the government, or the people, for each and every year, than the printing of both houses of Congress costs in ten years. If the printing were let out to the lowest bidder, or executed at a government office, the debates would not be printed as they are now. A daily newspaper, publishing the debates as full as the National Intelligencer and the Union are now publishing them, would sink from $7,500 to $12,000 a year; and I do not think that two editors could be found in the United States patriotic enough to sink that much money a year. If *one* could be found who would do it, he would probably so report the proceedings as to subserve his party, or some great manufacturing interest, which would pay him well for his support. If the government were to attempt to report the debates, a large minority if not majority of the people would repose but little confidence in the debates so published, as the reporters would be selected by the dominant party of Congress.[31]

In a general way, what Rives contended is true, but his conclusions need to be evaluated further to give an accurate picture of patronage and the political press. The Washington newspapers during the first half of the nineteenth century were much more than publications of record. Such newspapers as the *Intelligencer,*

[31]House Report 754, 29th Cong., 1st sess.

the *Globe,* and the *Union* did indeed provide excellent records of the debates and proceedings of Congress, but this was only part of their contribution. They also furnished keen analysis of the issues facing the federal government as well as a sharp delineation among the opposing viewpoints presented by various political factions within the nation. Note the daily dialogue among the leading party papers on such vital issues as western land policies, the Second United States Bank, the Specie Circular, the Mexican War, the internal improvements issue as well as nullification and states' rights. The space devoted to such issues was great. The analysis was deep. The thinking and debate were sharp. Because of opposing political philosophies on many of the issues, there was the constant debate of the issues which must have aided readers to understand these problems.

Political newspapers made no effort to observe that hobgoblin of twentieth-century journalism, objectivity. The administrative organ, with the exception of the *Intelligencer,* seldom made a pretense of explaining both sides of an issue. The duty of the administrative organ was to persuade, not to educate. Thus patronage contracts awarded by Congress made possible the publication of newspapers representing points of view other than those of the administration. With the aid of publishing some of the land office records, the editor of the *Telegraph,* for example, was able to remain on the Washington scene for six years after losing his administrative position, and during these years he effectively argued the viewpoint of the emerging sectionalists of the South. The *Intelligencer,* as mentioned earlier, published for 25 years after 1840 and presented a small minority voice in Washington. The *Intelligencer* continued to appear, although it never served as an administrative organ or received congressional printing work after the early years of the Harrison and Tyler administrations. Still the *Intelligencer* ably presented the moderate position to the end of the Civil War despite its lack of popularity and in the face of heavy circulation losses. Federal patronage made this possible.

The federal patronage system also allowed for a quality among the newspapers of the nation's capital which was found only rarely in other parts of the country. The editors, not dependent upon circulation for the main support of their papers, devoted a vastly greater share of their time and efforts to a more intellectual treatment of stories dealing with the nation's government and its workings. These were class newspapers of high intellectual quality that were never able to compete for circulation with the sensationalism of the penny press.

Probably one of the outstanding characteristics of the political editors during the first seven decades of American history under the United States Constitution was the policy-making function which many of the political editors exercised in both the administrative and congressional branches of the federal government. There is no doubt in the mind of any scholar who has studied the Jackson era that Blair was more than a political editor. He was a political adviser, and frequently his advice was the basis for a national policy. This was also true for other editors in other periods, including Gales and Seaton of the *National Intelligencer,* as well as Thomas Allen of the *Madisonian.* This same function was served in relation to Congress. The *Intelligencer* editors undoubtedly had a key role in formulating certain aspects of Whig policy and, in many instances, the *Intelligencer* office provided a caucus room for leading members of the party.

Even the way in which the political editors were treated by their contemporaries suggests their importance. They were accorded a high social status; their presence was welcomed at "entertainments" given by the great and powerful in politics during the first third of the nineteenth century. Similarly, high professional regard, special meetings, and visits were extended to the editors of this period by important visitors, both foreign and domestic, to the nation's capital.

The press was a part of the political apparatus of the country, serving not only as machinery of dissemination but also as an integral part of the creation of policies and messages which guided the country.

THE HISTORIAN AS SLEUTH: GRAFT, "GENTLEMEN'S AGREEMENTS," AND PUBLIC PRINTING

It is scarcely news that much, if not most of American history is taught upside-down and wrongside-out. Most history as taught emphasizes national politics, an emphasis that eighteenth- or nineteenth-century Americans would not have understood. Until the twentieth century, local, county, and state governments had more impact upon the everyday lives of most men and women than did the doings of the "leaders" in Washington, D.C. Similarly, journalism history has often had a decidedly Eastern and "national" tilt, with emphasis upon journalism in the national capitals (first Philadelphia, then Washington) or in financial and shipping capitals (first Boston, then New York).

In its relationships with government, the press—like the public— dealt primarily with municipal, county, and state governments. And this is true for the historian interested in looking at problems of economic support of the media (or searching for public printing scandals). The action was at the state and local level for much of American history, especially during the latter part of the nineteenth century. Take, for example, the notorious South Carolina printing frauds disclosed in 1876: Investigations discovered that the amount of money appropriated by South Carolina officials for public printing between 1868 and 1876 totaled more than $1.3 million. As Harold L. Nelson has pointed out, that amount was more than South Carolina had spent on printing in the 92 years between 1776 and 1868. State officers and legislators had used cooperative but crooked editors to channel funds out of government coffers and back into their own pockets.[32] Perhaps the South Carolina public officials and journalists were much more venal than their counterparts in other states. However, studies touching Washington, Wisconsin, Missouri, and Minnesota indicate that in a number of territories and states, the handling of public printing money was at least suspect, if not blatantly corrupt.[33]

Gyrations in securing public printing contracts at the state level were often something to behold. As one observer acidly remarked about public printing in the Washington Territory between 1853 and 1863, "fat offices are being freely dispensed." During that pe-

[32]Harold L. Nelson, *Freedom of the Press from Hamilton to the Warren Court* (Indianapolis, Ind., 1967), pp. 341–347.

[33]W. A. Katz, "Public Printers of Washington Territory, 1853–1863," *Pacific Northwest Quarterly* 51:3 (July 1960), 103–114; Alex Nagy, "Public Printing in Wisconsin Territory" (M.A. thesis, University of Wisconsin, 1970); William H. Taft, *Missouri Newspapers* (Columbia, Mo., 1964); Hage, *op. cit.*

riod, one printer bragged that he took in several thousand dollars doing one three-week job, and another paid a $2000 bribe to secure a printing contract.

Securing printing contracts was only part of the game. Again in the Washington Territory, one favorite maneuver involved printing far fewer copies of public documents than the number ordered by the legislature. Publishers were paid according to the number of copies of an item that were ordered, not by the number which they actually printed.

It is perhaps surprising that so little attention has been paid to public printing contracts: The records are often available. Furthermore, peculiar, if not downright fraudulent, practices have been described in such prominent places that it is rather startling that more journalism historians have not followed up such tips. Consider this passage from the famed *Autobiography of William Allen White,* discussing the county printing arrangements:

> The county printing was our reason for being. For that, we would sacrifice anything! For that, we wrangled and rowed with the other editors of the town and the county. The county printing was a major objective. In every western country newspaper in that golden day, the county printing, which amounted to five or six thousand dollars a year, was chiefly profit; and it was, as a matter of fact, almost our only profit.[34]

Years later, White explained to President Warren G. Harding how county printing contracts were awarded in his section of Kansas:

> I told him that there was a gentlemen's agreement between the Democratic paper and the [Emporia] Gazette that when the Democrats elected the county officers, whose business it was to let the county printing, we would not bid; or, if we did bid, we bid the full legal rate. So the Democrats let the printing to the Democratic paper. And when the county was Republican, the Democrats decently refrained from disturbing the legal rate by a cutthroat bid.[35]

In sum, it appears that much work remains to be done in tracing the way in which public printing contracts have been awarded at

[34]William Allen White, *The Autobiography of William Allen White* (New York, 1946), pp. 131–132.
    [35]*Ibid.,* p. 618.

all levels of government. A related, and fascinating, topic which deserves further investigation is the effect which holding public printing contracts had upon the content of newspaper reporting of governmental activities. Writing of the Washington Territory, W. A. Katz has declared that editors often repaid public printing contracts with editorial support: "Highly rhetorical, biased, and often libelous editorials supported the individual or party which has won the day for the editor."[36] Such servile gratitude for public printing revenues has not, however, always been the case. Many years earlier, during the War for Independence, newspapermen often found enough independence to live up to printer Eleazer Oswald's bravely defiant goal: "[A] constant Examination into the Characters of Ministers and Magistrates should be . . . promoted and encouraged."[37] More examination into the conflict between principle and profit in the history of American journalism is clearly needed.

GOVERNMENT AND THE PRESS:
A CHANGED RELATIONSHIP

The impact of industrialization changed the relationship between government and the mass media. Mass circulation and commercial advertising shifted the dependence of the press from the political parties and government to big business and a mass audience. The proceedings of government became only a small part of the content of mass circulation papers as publications changed from productions of relatively high intellectual content to papers aimed at catering to lower—if not lowest—common denominators.

Mass media became, in effect, part of big business. They were supported by big business; they spoke for big business. The press transformed itself into the spokesman for the new industrial capitalism which fastened itself upon the United States during the latter decades of the nineteenth century and with religious fervor turned to subduing nature for the advantage of man, or, at least, certain men. Under such an acquisitive system, government became a threat to the fulfillment of dreams of exploitating the nation's resources, both physical and human. Government became, in the eyes

[36]Katz, *op. cit.*, p. 104.
[37]Quoted in Teeter, *op. cit.*, p. 451.

of many newspaper publishers, the chief threat to freedom of action of the industrial capitalists and, perhaps of necessity, to freedom of the press. To underwrite such a change, business, through advertising, replaced government as the supporting agent. Government evolved from active institutional and financial support of the press to a kind of acquiescence: tolerating expression about the governmental processes.

But the change in financial base has had other far-reaching effects. News in a political newspaper was interpreted for the reader from a particular philosophical basis. Happenings were reported in terms of meaning to a particular political party. Once these political philosophies were removed, the criterion for selection of political news, and other news for that matter, became unclear. Wire services were forced to serve those of all political persuasions. Each reader increasingly was left to decide for himself what a particular political action may have meant, although reporters may well have been far better informed and better able to explain the significance of a political act.

The political process was the one means by which a citizen could participate in his government and in many aspects of society. Yet the press, dominated by the business community, had in many ways become the arbiter of what political information the citizen would receive. And as yet with no continuing means of press appraisal and study, the citizen would have to assume that he was receiving the information he needed to participate responsibly in the political process of the nation.

Government patronage, of course, did not end suddenly or even completely during the nineteenth century. Even after the Washington, D.C., papers were cut off from congressional and other printing contracts, newspapers throughout the nation, as suggested earlier, continued to be financed by local, state, and federal treasuries. Even today, government supports continue in the form of postal subsidies and legal advertising.

During the twentieth century the relationships between press and government and between the press and the political parties have undergone even more far-reaching changes. The press, indeed, has become an *observer* rather than a participant in the political processes of the country. Gone are the days when a newspaper boasted of adhering to a particular philosophy which it espoused both in its news columns and on its editorial pages. Every person had to be considered a potential subscriber and no sizable member of them could be offended. Advertisers paid the bill and demanded a product offering something to everyone. The press moved out of the councils of government and into the carnivals of commerce, away from ideology toward what the press deceptively termed objectivity—whatever that meant. Offense to no one was a strategy; commitment to no philosophy evidently was often perceived as a necessity.

With this change in role also came an enormous change in content. Entertainment, human-interest items, sports, crossword puzzles, and comics replaced the diet of political news which editors, during the early decades of the nineteenth century, had published for their subscribers. Government became just another source to compete for space along with the race track and the test kitchen. In the twentieth century, government has hired thousands of professionals to collect and write news *for* reporters employed by the mass media. In many ways, government was more of a participant in the news dissemination process than it had ever been in the past, but not at the financial level. Somehow, if the financial base of the press was separated from government, and if enough cries of "managed news" were raised, the press could still be said to be free. But perhaps other assessments should be heard.

As V. O. Key argued in *Public Opinion and American Democracy*:

> The partisan press put a degree of order into the confusing world of politics. The modern press tends to convey all its disorders. Only the best informed reader, who also happens to read one of the best papers, can place events into a meaningful scheme. In a sense, the press has moved from the role of actor to that of narrator.[38]

Independence is what many term the political role into which the press has evolved in order to gain economic advantage. But have the mass media really ceased to pay homage to government, despite the severing of the old political-economic ties? True, "press lords" like to see themselves as critics of government and guardians of liberty within the nation. But some observers think that whatever

[38]V. O. Key, *Public Opinion and American Democracy* (New York, 1961), p. 393.

is left of the much-touted "watchdog function" of the media today is really much more a small, yapping bark than a fierce, toothy bite. As columnist Joseph Kraft has asserted:

> It may be presumptuous to say [with Douglass Cater] that the press is a "fourth branch of government," but the two are certainly intertwined. In the typical Washington situation, news is not nosed out by keen reporters and then purveyed to the public. It is manufactured inside the government, by various interested parties for purposes of their own, and then put out to the press in ways and at times that suit the source.[39]

Viewed in such a gloomy context, it can be seen that the study of the political-economic past of the mass media matters a great deal, if only to gain more perspective on how government and communications media powers intermingle. Someone once suggested that history is an attempt to find the correct answers to equations which have been half-erased. The economic side of the equation, where press and government intersect, is for the most part only dimly seen by communications history. Large scale "correct answers" may always elude the historian, but far more data are available than is reflected in print to date. Such political-economic study may never be able to fill in the gaps left by many years of neglect, but perhaps, in the future, the sins of omission may be absolved to some extent by patient research. More can be learned about media revenues, about circulation patterns, and about the financial interrelationships between government and the mass media. It now remains to be seen whether what *can* be done *will* be done.

[39]Joseph Kraft, *Profiles in Power: A Washington Insight* (New York, 1966), p. 93.

4 TECHNOLOGY: FREEDOM FOR WHAT?

Donald L. Shaw

Donald L. Shaw, University of North Carolina,
has headed the bibliography project of the
History Division of the Association for Education
in Journalism since 1966. He has written
articles on many facets of mass communications
and is editor of *Journalism Abstracts.*

Technology, thank God, has freed man; it also has
enslaved him, or very nearly promises to do so. It is
exhilarating to live in an age in which man has gone
to the moon and transplanted human hearts from
the dead to the living. But it is also distressing to live
with polluted air and water, crowded highways and
skyways, and constant industrial noise. The rewards of
technological development are great but the price is
often high.

From the first, man has developed tools to cope with the challenge of his immediate environment. He has built tools to help him with hunting, fishing, agriculture, animal husbandry, and mining, through manufacturing, transportation, means of communication, medicine, and military technology. In this way, he mastered the other creatures. Broadly defined, technologies are the cultural traditions developed in human communities for dealing with the physical and biological environment, including the human biological organism. Man always has applied knowledge for practical ends.[1] This general technological and practical use of knowledge (to reduce hand labor and produce an improved product) is reflected in the historical development of mass communications—an integral and important part of the larger American experience. We should briefly examine the important framework provided for mass communications by this general experience.

PROMISE AND PERIL OF TECHNOLOGY IN AMERICAN LIFE

The "father of history," Herodotus, who lived in the fifth century B.C., was impressed by the speed of the news service of the Persian kings. Messengers on horseback could travel 250 miles in 36 hours, about seven miles an hour. This speed remained the norm until the invention of complex machines and motors in the nineteenth century. In communication, the two technological triumphs most characteristic of our age are long-distance communication and transportation faster than the speed of sound.[2]

These are, of course, only part of the tremendous technological changes which are the continuing legacy of the industrial revolution that started in Europe and spread to our shores in the early nineteenth century. Today when we think of "progress" we most likely think in technological terms—that is, about *things* not ideas.

[1]Robert S. Merrill, "The Study of Technology," in David L. Sills, ed., *International Encyclopedia of the Social Sciences* (New York, 1968), p. 576.

[2]Heinz Gartmann, *Man Unlimited* (New York, 1957), p. 8; and Claude M. Blair, "The Challenge of Technology in Communications," in Alex Edelstein, ed., "The Challenge of Communications in Century 21," *Journalism Quarterly*, Special Supplement, Summer 1963, p. 421.

Indeed, what does it mean to say an *idea* "progresses" (except for certain scientific concepts)? Ideas change; things—cars, television sets, toasters—get "better."

In bending ideas to fit machines, we surely have accomplished much. In 1850, machines did about 35 percent of industrial and farm work while man did 13 percent and animals the rest. Today man and animals do only 2 percent; our machines do the rest. Machines have extended man's arms, created jobs (and taken them away), and allowed us free time unimaginable a century ago.

Our technological processes and machines have provided us with better housing, enriched diets, improved medical services. We have synthetic rubber and fabrics and improved processes for hardening steels. Plastics now have replaced wood, metals, and porcelain (sometimes for the better) on many products. How could one begin to list everything?

Technology has brought lower prices and often higher quality through automation and mass production, in which a worker—or machine—has only a small part in the finished product. Mass production, which Eli Whitney initiated in 1800 with musket production for the fledgling U.S. Army, is one of the most significant industrial developments of all times, affecting all industries including mass communications. It was the beginning of the end of craftsmanship.

Since the end of World War II, the development of computers with amazing capacity for high-speed information processing has accelerated technological developments. We have built control mechanisms so that machines can speak, control, pace, and "feed back" information to each other. Cybernetics, the study of control mechanisms and information transfer, has become an important science with wide applications. It has helped put man on the moon as well as remove almost all men from at least some production lines. Since 1951, for example, the two Brooks Park engine plants of Ford Motor Company have been producing six-cylinder engine blocks from rough castings in a totally automated process. The castings are first produced in an automated foundry before being fed into a process where 42 automatic machines perform 53 precision cutting operations and borings. The result, in 14.6 minutes, is a finished engine block. From start to finish, no operator touches a part. As one Ford machine operator once put it, "I don't do nothing but press these two buttons." Sometimes, he said, he used his thumbs, sometimes his wrists or whole arm.[3] One is reminded of Hannah Arendt's point that it is possible to strengthen tools, multiplying human strength to the point of almost replacing it. In some production processes we are already there.[4]

John Platt recently estimated the changes of the past century:

> [We] have increased our speeds of communication by a factor of 10^7; our speeds of travel by 10^2; our speeds of data handling by 10^6; our energy resources by 10^3; our power of weapons by 10^6; our ability to control diseases by something like 10^2; and our rate of population growth to 10^3 times what it was a few thousand years ago.[5]

This has not occurred in a vacuum. Large backwaters of people—for example, blacks and those in the Appalachian area—have not acquired the skills to participate in the new age or they have been replaced by machines. Others have entered a new era of affluence and free time. Both groups are part of the modern mass audience of public communications.

But while the average man has never had more time to play, to interact with his environment, he never has been more isolated from the immediate *personal* environmental challenges which bring meaning when met and overcome. Man's history is a long saga of difficulties overcome and emergencies met. This contributed an atmosphere of adventure, danger, expectancy—the kind of exhilaration which helps free man from himself and bondage to things and enables him to reach for abstract higher values. Accumulation of goods alone does not seem to make up for the loss of this exhilaration and the mass media have filled the void with uncertain success.[6]

[3]From John Diebold, "The Nature of Automation," in John G. Burke, ed., *The New Technology and Human Values* (Belmont, Calif., 1966), p. 113. This book is an excellent compilation of articles dealing with technology, particularly the social impact.

[4]Hannah Arendt, *The Human Condition* (Chicago, 1958), p. 122.

[5]John Platt, "What We Must Do," *Science 166* (November 28, 1969), 1115–1121.

[6]The interpretation in this section borrows in part from René Dubos, "Modern Horsemen of the Apocalypse," in Burke, *New Technology*, pp. 304 ff.

Today man still faces dangerous challenges from the environment; indeed, he is nearly strangled from impure air and water. He may spend much of his life commuting to distant suburbs where he may still gasp for a breath of fresher air. Yet many of these dangers result from impersonal forces and institutions in society upon which it is all too difficult for the individual to impose change. In an earlier age, it was simpler to shoot menacing animals and probably more fun.

Automation and dial watching eliminate physical labor hardships but monotonous environments and mechanical operations have their own deleterious effects on the human brain and motivation. Some psychological studies have shown that prolonged exposure to a monotonous situation results in impairment of mental processes. An individual shows childish emotional responses, his visual perception becomes distorted, he sees hallucinations, and his brain wave patterns change. In short, the very efficiency of industrial production has created a pathology of boredom. The choice of using one's thumbs or one's arm can hardly be viewed as provocative.

Furthermore, the boredom is relatively unrelieved. One rarely gets creatively involved *as an individual* in making anything important. So economically integrated is our age that for most the extent of our production involvement is growing a garden, building a piece of furniture, or, perhaps, constructing a model airplane. We rarely can see *ourselves* in a product. Of course, we can escape into even harder work, or, as do millions, we can turn to newspapers, television, or magazines to construct an accurate picture of the environment. But unfortunately we are constrained from making much impact *as individuals* on our environment.

Of course, we can consume the abundant products of the technological society. With only 6 percent of the world's population, the United States in 1966 consumed 34 percent of the world's energy production, 29 percent of all steel production, and 17 percent of all timber cut.[7] Much of the timber was used in pulp paper production to keep newspaper and magazine presses revolving. And for the press, as for society, the freedom and constraints imposed by technological development have become ever more evident.

[7]Estimates of Luther J. Carter, "The Population Crisis: Rising Concern at Home," *Science 166* (November 7, 1969), 722–726.

FREEDOM AND CONSTRAINT OF THE PRESS— THE HISTORICAL DEVELOPMENT

Nineteenth-century technological developments turned the press into a mass audience medium. Publishers (printers then) found themselves freed from the tedious constraints of a hand press and as the century matured into old age and a new century took its place, they found technological changes also could impose new constraints, create new problems to challenge us.

If Gutenberg had walked into a print shop in 1800 he would have felt at home. Since the fifteenth century there had been little change in type and composition methods; in fact, paper was generally lower in quality than in his time. While presses had gained by various modifications, Gutenberg still would have had to apply ink to type forms with leather daubers.[8]

But printing soon shared in the advances of the industrial revolution. From 1811–1813, a Saxon journeyman printer, Frederick Koenig, made the first effective break with the classical "wine press" construction. He applied steam power and developed a press with an impression cylinder. The English manufacturer, David Napier, further refined the cylinder idea. By 1830, the New York firm of R. Hoe and Company produced a flat bed and cylinder press and by 1832 had one which could print 4000 impressions an hour. In Gutenberg's time, printers could turn out about 600 impressions a day. We suddenly had entered a new age. Hoe and other companies continued development of better presses; by the early twentieth century presses could produce 72,000 32-page newspapers an hour.

While the development of high-speed presses probably is the major technological advancement of the nineteenth century, other developments were almost as important. One was the improved process for paper making. Obviously, the fast new presses voraciously consumed paper. In 1799, N. L. Robert patented a paper-making machine—the Fourdrinier—which put into practice principles employed today. Further developments in the 1840s resulted in a process by which wood pulp could be made into paper. By the

[8]Three excellent sources for general technological developments are Alfred McClung Lee, *The Daily Newspaper in America* (New York, 1937); Edwin Emery, *The Press and America* (Englewood Cliffs, N.J., 1962); and Frank Luther Mott, *American Journalism* (New York, 1962).

1860s, with still further refinements, paper production had outgrown the handicraft stage and become big business.

Improved presses and paper production methods enabled the newspapers to reach larger masses and helped to create the Penny Press of the 1830s. However, the telegraph, which newspapers began using in the 1840s to bring in timely outside news, had an enormous impact on news values. The telegraph, with its emphasis on many concise, short messages (long ones were expensive) and rapidity, significantly enlarged the horizons of American readers and further whetted eager appetites for timely news. Doubtless also the telegraph played a role in unifying the diversely peopled and expanding America into a nation. As the nation strung railroads over the land, telegraph lines followed to carry news (and control railroad traffic flow, of course). Where new settlers went, and news could be sent, newspapers soon followed. In 1845–1856 in Illinois, 30 dailies sprang up with the appearance of the telegraph.

By the middle of the nineteenth century, the process of stereotyping—the casting of plates for printing from molds—revolutionized advertising. The necessity for column rules to hold type-revolving presses together gave way. One could advertise in whole pages, not just single columns. Many newspapers also began using "patent insides," pages upon which news and features already had been printed at some other plant. This particularly helped struggling smaller newspapers, especially weeklies, to carry more diverse materials at reduced costs.

Typewriters attained popularity in newspapers offices about 1878 after Remington equipped them to print with both upper- and lower-case letters. In 1877, the telephone, which Alexander Graham Bell invented two years earlier, was drafted for use in sending newspaper dispatches. In terms of news transmission, the telephone soon became an important supplement to the telegraph. The diffusion was rapid; there were 54,000 telephones in 1880 and more than 7,500,000 in 1910. By the early 1960s, the figure reached more than 80 million —430 phones for every 1000 people—and close to half the world's telephones were in the United States.

In 1886, the first casting of a line of type for a newspaper was made in the *New York Tribune* plant on Ottmar Mergenthaler's Linotype machine. This was, and is, a very important development and this machine, with modifications, can be found today in many newspaper plants. Now it competes with the newer and often cheaper techniques of computer composition, but it greatly simplified and speeded up the mechanical processing of news by virtually doubling the production speed.

The improvement of the vacuum tube by Lee De Forest in 1906 opened the way for voice broadcasting and, in the 1920s, the first American stations to seek regular public listenership made their bow. The vacuum tube more recently has given way to the transistor and the miniaturization of electric circuitry, a development which has reduced production costs and made possible the wide distribution of radio and television sets to world masses. Ninety-eight percent of American homes have at least one usable radio; the average is about four per family. Of the approximately 262 million radios in the United States, almost 65 million are in autos.

In 1927, Bell Telephone laboratories publicly demonstrated black and white television and two years later showed what color would add. Since World War II, television has taken its place in most American homes along with newspapers, radio, and—in many—books and magazines. The diffusion of television sets in America has been phenomenal. In 1948, there were one million sets in use but there were 17 million only four years later. In 1966, the total approached 70 million, and more than nine of ten American homes had at least one set. Family members, singly or collectively, viewed television more than 20 hours a week, a sizable portion of waking time.

Here one merely can touch on some major technological changes but it is clear that the technological developments of the nineteenth and twentieth centuries helped create an electronic and print mass media capable of quick diffusion of information or entertainment to enormous audiences. We *cannot* escape.

It is also clear that the mass media are far from the small, often isolated, print and newspaper shops which once characterized American public communication. Technology, in freeing the press from this smallness and isolation has brought new problems to mass media. *They* cannot escape.

Newspapers and magazines became big business in the late nineteenth century; their growth generally paralleled changes in American business and industry during the period. Technological innovations increased the financial responsibilities and risks for both large and small publishers. It certainly cost money to buy type-setting machines, engraving plants, and high-speed presses. Further-more, the publisher who wanted to keep abreast of the changes had to constantly increase circulation and advertising revenue.

This is not to say that technology accounted for everything. As immigrants (and those leaving farms) crowded into cities, news-papers found large new audiences. Newspapers also served an im-portant role, publication of information to socially integrate the new people into the emerging American urban society. Many eagerly read to acquire knowledge of their new surroundings; some used news-papers to find jobs, others simply tried to learn how to read Eng-lish. With growth of cities came the development of large retail stores which advertised in newspapers. This revenue source helped free newspapers from financial handouts—hence control—of purely political interest groups. The large daily press was necessarily an urban phenomenon.

But the new technology threatened older, agrarian-centered val-ues. It was possible to feel ambiguous about rapid changes. The nineteenth century was, as one scholar beautifully described it, "a time in which man was striving to preserve individual values and at the same time cheering the advance of the individual-destroying machine, living in a civilization which though dominated by rural and agrarian values was doomed to yield to the 'iron men,' the factories, and the slums."[9] This analysis still applies, but we are more uncertain in what sense our machines are "advancing."

In short, the press was initiated fully as a *major economic insti-tution* of American life. This meant the press was necessarily con-strained by marketplace mechanisms; however, it was no longer at the beck and call of a particular politician or party group. J. Edward Gerald, a perceptive communications scholar, has summarized it bluntly:

> The agencies of mass communication . . . are economic institu-tions. In the hands of the men who control them they are, first and last, business firms. The writing journalist has had a lion's share of attention in the life and literature of journalism, but the

[9]Calder M. Pickett, "Technology and the New York Press in the 19th Century," *Journalism Quarterly* 37:3 (Summer 1960), 399.

0

place set aside within the firms and the industry for the writers and editors—no matter how it may be semi-insulated by custom and practice from the counting room—is shaped by what happens to the finished product in the market place. Internal changes of any kind in a firm, whether proposed by outside or inside groups, will be agreed upon, in the final analysis, only when they have been fitted into a budget, a cost record and a balance sheet.[10]

Thundering editorial voices which had dominated the newspapers of the early nineteenth century softened—became stilled on some papers—as the newspaper began to emphasize news over opinion. By the 1870s news held stage center and on most larger papers there was an expansion and specialization of news staffs and a quickening of news-gathering activities. At the same time, the rising complexity of the news operation spawned a new, highly skilled managerial corps.

The newspapers which had once spoken with a tiny voice to a small number of people lost this unique quality. With the help of technological developments, they became institutionalized and somehow more distant, less personal. Wire services, which sent news by telegraph, especially accelerated this trend. By the late nineteenth century, the news supplied by wire services was the only regular outside source used by many papers. Because substantially the same news was sent to all papers, newspapers which once were clearly distinguishable by editorial tone and make-up began to look alike. Standardization, the bane of the current press, spread. Furthermore, the press-service news style—the inverted pyramid organization—had such an impact on the way news was written by local reporters that all news soon began to look similar in style.

The use of wire-service news, plus the growing size of the press, helped increase distance between press and reader; it was a natural development. At the same time, the news columns filled with wire news from distant places undoubtedly extended horizons of readers, but where editors chose to use wire copy rather than to hire reporters to cover the local scene, the result was really *insulation* of the reader from much of the significance of local life.

[10]J. Edward Gerald, "Economic Research and the Mass Media," *Journalism Quarterly* 35 (Winter 1958), 49–50.

IMPACT OF THE TELEGRAPH:
A WISCONSIN CASE STUDY

The impact of the telegraph on the press can be examined more closely, at least for one state, by reference to a study by the author. The study sought to trace the decline of political news bias in the reporting of national Presidential campaign news in the Wisconsin English-language daily press from 1852 through 1916 and to see how much of that decline could be attributed to increasing use of relatively unbiased political news from press association wire news and other factors.[11]

Historians previously had observed a decline in partisanship and political news bias in the last part of the nineteenth and early twentieth centuries and had attributed it to a number of causes, particularly (1) increasing use of relatively unbiased wire news; (2) increasing unbanization (enlarging circulation) resulting in more revenue sources from readers and advertising from the sprawling retail stores; (3) declining power of political parties; (4) increasing professionalization—with the implication of an ethical basis of conduct—on the part of newsmen, editors, and publishers; and (5) declining competition from other papers—hence the growing need for exercise of greater responsibility by the remaining papers to insure adequate, fair news coverage.

The study developed an operational definition of news bias and employed content analysis to examine a random sample of 147 Wisconsin English-language daily papers for Octobers of 1852–1916 national election years. A total of 1097 Presidential campaign stories—those stories with a Presidential or Vice-Presidential candidate as a referent—were coded as "biased" or "unbiased." Coders also recorded how the story came to the paper, whether from the telegraph, the papers' own reporters, or from other sources.

The study's operational bias definition was a traditional one based on value-laden words—adjectives, adverbs, verbs—inserted in the

[11]This section is based on Donald L. Shaw, "Bias in the News: A Study of National Presidential Campaign Coverage in the Wisconsin English Daily Press 1852–1916" (Ph.D. diss., University of Wisconsin, 1966); Donald L. Shaw, "News Bias and the Telegraph: a Study of Historical Change," *Journalism Quarterly* 44:1 (Spring 1967), 3–12, 31; and Donald L. Shaw, "The Nature of Campaign News in the Wisconsin Press 1852–1916," *Journalism Quarterly* 45:2 (Summer 1968), 326–329.

story in such a way that the overall impression created was a positive or negative—rather than neutral—feeling toward the story referent. After completion of coding for each sampled year, each paper was assigned a bias score. If a newspaper issue carried more biased than unbiased stories it was assigned a score of 3, representing "high bias." If a newspaper issue contained an equal number of biased and unbiased stories, it was assigned a score of 2, "balanced on bias." If a paper carried more unbiased than biased Presidential campaign news stories, it was assigned a score of 1, or "low bias." For each year, scores for each sampled paper represent an average of the bias scores for all issues sampled of that paper. (Papers were very stable from issue to issue.) The study demonstrated that Presidential campaign news bias dropped in the 1852–1916 period, as historians had noted, but that it fell dramatically between the 1880 and 1884 period, a *sudden* drop unnoticed by historians of Wisconsin.

Table 1 summarizes the major findings. It shows the 1880–1884 period as a kind of "watershed" for the Wisconsin English-language daily press. From 1884 through 1916, the sampled papers never reached the same levels of news bias as in earlier years. Why had biased news declined so suddenly?

A technological phenomenon, the telegraph, is the answer. The news coming in by telegraph *was* less biased than that provided by the papers' own reporters or that from news stories clipped from other papers or news from other sources. Furthermore, there was a large increase in wire service news between 1880 and 1884. In 1852–1880 the study found that wire news accounted for 18 percent of the total number of Presidential campaign stories, but in the 1884–1916 period the proportion jumped to 84 percent. The relative amount of news carried by the sample newspapers' own reporters declined about as sharply as the rise in amount of wire news. In the 1852–1880 period, the sample papers' reporters accounted for 45 percent of the total number of campaign stories but in the 1884–1916 years only 12 percent. None of the other types of outside news in the period—such as letters to the editor or stories clipped from other papers—accounted for a significant proportion of Presidential campaign coverage in the 1884–1916 period, yet in the 1852–1880 years, these sources had accounted for more than 37 percent of the total number of campaign news stories.

Table 1

Bias Means for All Sample Newspapers for Presidental Election Years 1852–1916

ELECTION YEARS	BIAS MEANS	TOTAL NO. STORIES	NO. SAMPLE PAPERS
1852	1.75	30	4
1856	2.57	10	7
1860	1.85	41	9
1864	1.64	30	7
1868	1.86	45	7
1872	2.45	56	7
1876	2.22	70	12
1880	1.92	38	10
1884	1.00[a]	61	4
1888	1.04	82	8
1892	1.48	29	9
1896	1.08	143	13
1900	1.04	101	9
1904	1.14	31	7
1908	1.06	113	9
1912	1.12	117	14
1916	1.26	100	11
	X = 1.53	T = 1097	T = 147

[a]Note the sharp bias decline between 1880 and 1884.

There were at least two reasons why the number of wire stories printed showed such a sudden increase. First, the increase in miles of wire from 1880 (233,534) to 1884 (430,571) was larger than any other increase during a four-year interval from 1868 through 1900. Second, this was the time when Western Union put important technological developments into general operation. The Duplex, a device that permits two messages to be transmitted simultaneously in opposite directions on one wire was perfected, and soon came the Quadruplex, which allowed four messages to be sent simultaneously, two in each direction, on a single wire. The effect of these and other developments was to make more wire news available to more newspapers about the time of the 1880s. At the same time there was a decline in the price of telegraph news (as it became easier and cheaper to send more of it) and in newsprint price.

Furthermore, the significant increase in wire news seemed to dominate other historical explanatory factors related to declining political news bias in the Wisconsin press. The data were quantified so as to permit comparison of bias scores of newspapers on the basis of amount of circulation, competition, and advertising carried and on the basis of the size of the area it served. Hence, for the Wisconsin English-language press, one can see that increased advertising and circulation and reduced competition from other English-language papers (as papers consolidated and/or went out of business) *did* result in lower news bias, as one would expect from observations about the general declining bias in American journalism during the period. For example, if greater advertising frees a newspaper from dependence on political handouts, then one would expect lower bias from newspapers with greater advertising. Newspapers in communities with large or rapidly growing populations should be responsive to new, unpolitical audience sources and should be freer from news bias, as should those with larger circulation.

Therefore, year by year from 1852 through 1916, the study broke the newspapers into high and low groups (using the median) for each of these predictor, or locator, variables (amount of circulation, advertising, etc.). Table 2 summarizes the major findings according to the two time periods the study found significant.

While the table shows there were two statistically significant differences (area of circulation and competition) in the early period, there were no such differences later. It was as if the telegraph had wiped out any further basis for differences. In the early period newspapers serving areas with larger population *were* lower on bias, as expected; at the same time, those with higher competition were *lower* on bias. One would have expected more bias or sensationalism in order to attract a larger audience in the competitive situation. It may have been that low-competition newspapers tended to allow freer reign for news bias because there were few or no local competitors to "call their hand" or because editors in these towns felt they had to reflect community consensus as they saw it. Although not shown in the table, papers did not differ on news bias regardless of whether they claimed political party affiliation or political

Table 2

Significance of Historical Locator Variables Before and After the Major Impact of Telegraph News in Wisconsin English-language Daily Press, 1852–1916

COMMUNITY AND NEWSPAPER VARIABLES	1852–1880	1884–1916
COMMUNITY		
Area with Large vs. Small Population	Sig.[a]	N.S.
Area with Large vs. Small Pop. Growth	N.S.	N.S.
Area with High vs. Low Competition	Sig.[b]	N.S.
NEWSPAPERS		
Papers with Large vs. Small Circulation	N.S.[c]	N.S.
Papers with Large vs. Small Advertising	N.S.	N.S.

[a]Newspapers serving areas with large population were lower on political news bias.

[b]Newspapers serving areas with high competition were lower on political news bias.

[c]Comparisons for the early period are from 1872 through 1880 because of the difficulty in obtaining circulation figures for the earlier years.

independence. In short, the findings suggest technological determinism as at least a partial explanation for declining political news bias. Nor is that all.

Telegraph news also appeared to influence press methods and philosophy. After the sharp decline in political news bias resulting from increased use of wire news there was a slower, but parallel, drop in news bias in *all* Presidential campaign news regardless of whether written by the papers' own reporters or clipped from stories in other newspapers or from other sources. Since the bias decline started only after 1884, it suggests that reporters learned to imitate the relatively unbiased news style of the wire services. Further, in the late 1880s and early 1890s, one could find rather frequent references, in the reports of annual meetings of the Wisconsin Press Association, to the social responsibility of the press and to journalism as a "profession." In 1889, for the first time in Wisconsin, an editor at the annual meeting of the state press association called for the formal establishment of the "ethics of our profession." This was just before the muckrakers and others began to reexamine American political and economic institutions. They found room for much improvement and there was growing concern about the ethical underpinnings of many groups and institutions in our society. But it is still interesting that—in Wisconsin at least—the direct attacks on libertarianism, a philosophy allowing free reign to expression of the publisher's opinions, and the promotion of social responsibility *followed* the clearly established drop in political news bias (i.e., technologically "enforced" responsible reporting) by almost a decade.

The abundant wire news also altered political "reality" by 1884 and after. The study showed the origins of political news stories were concentrated heavily in Wisconsin or immediately surrounding states in 1852–1880 and included many speeches or reports by supporters of Presidential candidates rather than by the candidates themselves. After 1884, however, stories were much more often about the candidate himself (what he was doing or saying) regardless of where the candidate might be. Readers, in other words, were moved more directly to the event.

This is precisely where readers wanted to be, in touch with the news shortly after it happened. Wire news enlarged the daily newspaper coverage area to the entire world and heightened desire for timeliness.

Hence, while wire news appeared to be related to declining news bias in the Wisconsin press, it may have affected basic journalistic writing and press philosophy as well as altered the shape of political reality for Wisconsin readers.[12]

INNIS, McLUHAN— A LARGER VIEW OF TECHNOLOGICAL IMPACT

Marshall McLuhan, who with his fellow Canadian scholar Harold A. Innis, has speculated on the relationship between technologies and the historical (Innis) and current (McLuhan) human experience. McLuhan has focused wide public attention on the relationship between television and reader/viewer perceptions and has raised interesting questions about the impact of our technological experience.

For Innis and McLuhan, the history of mass communications is central to the history of Western civilization, but while they both argue for the centrality of communication technologies, they operate from profoundly different premises. Innis argues that mass media

[12]One way it did so was to virtually ignore minor party candidates.

provide a way of explaining the development of Western civilization, of explicating key causal relationships in the growth and spread of national power on a worldwide basis. More directly, a civilization is free to extend only to the limits allowed by available communication means. "Time-binding" media—such as parchment, clay, or stone—are difficult to transport, hence they constrain the ability of a society to reach out beyond its own present and past. By contrast, "space-binding" media—for example, paper and papyrus—are light and, therefore, can be moved easily across space in a reasonably short time without great message distortion. Obviously, such media in the hands of the Romans might lead to growth of an empire. Such media, in fact, are a necessary, but of course not sufficient, means for such empire growth.[13]

A given communication medium will shape basic social structures in a society because it favors growth of certain kinds of interests at the expense of others. For example, societies constrained by time-binding media necessarily are based on oral traditions, handed down from father to son, emphasizing present and past rather than future. Societies with the ability to communicate rapidly and easily tend to emphasize spacial relations and to focus on the future (particularly the future of empire) rather than the present and past. Or, as Professor James W. Carey of the University of Illinois puts it, "Whereas the character of storage and reception of the oral tradition favor continuity over time, the written tradition favors discontinuity in time through continuity over space."[14] But the basic point here is that the technological limits, or constraints, of a given period *bias* (Innis's term) the basic structure of civilization and in fact limit or free man in any efforts to reach beyond himself to other civilizations (beyond his own past).

While Innis concentrates on the effects of communications technologies on social organization and culture, McLuhan cites perception and sensory organization as its principal effects. McLuhan, in short, concentrates on perception and thought, deemphasizing institutions; for Innis, it is the reverse. For McLuhan, all men

[13]The section is based primarily on Harold A. Innis, *The Bias of Communication* (Toronto, 1951); Marshall McLuhan, *Understanding Media* (New York, 1964); and James W. Carey, "Harold Adams Innis and Marshall McLuhan," *The Antioch Review* 27 (Spring 1967), 5–39.

[14]James W. Carey, *op. cit.,* p. 12.

stand symbiotically related to all media—the media in fact extend the sensory capacities of man. Furthermore, the media, by extending man's perceptual sensitivities, influence his picture of reality. Speech, of course, was the first extension of man's sensory capacities, but man's senses extend to the limits of the medium of communication dominating a culture—e.g., television for us.

Or, as Carey summarizes the core of McLuhan's argument: "Media of communication . . . are vast social metaphors that not only transmit information but determine what is knowledge, that not only orient us to the world but tell us what kind of world exists, that not only excite and delight our sense but by altering the ratio of sensory equipment which we use actually change our character."[15] It especially is television—a "cool" medium (one which demands viewer involvement)—which dramatically has altered the "mix" of our senses. Whereas print imposed linearity and order on reality—we have to read from left to right, for example—television's coolness freights no such requirement. In American television, the scanning (the system of lines which crisscross the screen to form the image) is low definition, as compared to movies. The viewer therefore must get *involved,* must himself fill in auditory, visual, and tactile cues to "complete" the tube's not-quite-filled-in message. Cool media in brief involve *all* the senses because they call for active participation of the consumer.

In this sense, it is rather unlike reading. It is more like the audio dependent tribe whose culture Innis described. McLuhan has argued that the print culture is dead, that we are "retribalizing," that we have created a new generation of young, involved people who want to *touch, feel, handle* life. In short, total involvement. If so (but probably not, because of the perceptual simplicity of the McLuhan argument), communication technologies are nerve-deep in our bodies. What else can communication technologies do?

VISION OF THE FUTURE, LEGACY OF THE PAST

In the future, communication technologies will most likely continue their accelerated development. In 1965, the Communications

15James W. Carey, *op. cit.,* p. 18.

Satellite Corporation (Comsat) of the United States launched Early Bird, the first commercial communications satellite. An active satellite with 240 telephone channels, it could, and has, carried live broadcasts between the United States and Europe. Before the end of this new decade, transatlantic satellites will provide some 42,000 simultaneous voice-data channels or 24 full-time color television channels, and eventually, the laser beam will provide nearly unlimited communication capacity.

Development is not limited to television. Facsimile—high-speed electronic reproduction in different locations—has enabled the *Wall Street Journal* and *Christian Science Monitor* to approximate national newspapers. At the same time, the AP and UPI have experimented with transmission of different versions of a story to editors who view (and edit) the story on a screen before ordering production of a tape to be fed to conventional typesetters.

The computer is creeping into the newsroom. Dean Wayne A. Danielson, of the University of Texas School of Communication, has explored uses of the computer for writing and editing. "This may startle you," he said in 1964, "but I believe that one of the decisions you are going to have to make about the computer tide is this: do you want to have some of your news stories written by machines?" He suggests that the computer can be used to write routine, standardized stories like weddings and obituaries.[16]

The development of cold-type composition methods has enabled many newspapers to shuck heavy, cumbersome, and sometimes antiquated composing equipment. As an added advantage, cold-type composition does not require as highly skilled (or highly paid) operators as linotype did, and is more compatible (and cheaper) for use with offset printing. These new methods provide some promise of returning competition to some small- and medium-sized city newspapers.

The restoration of competition has vitally concerned many. Daily newspaper competition has declined steadily since 1880. Nixon and Ward have shown that the total number of noncompetitive cities for selected years from 1880 to 1960 was as follows: 1880, 150; 1920, 743; 1940, 1245; and 1960, 1400. There was a corresponding

[16]Wayne A. Danielson, "How Computer Technology Will Affect the Newsroom" (Paper presented at the University of Wisconsin Journalism Institutes, Madison, May 8, 1964).

decline in the number of cities with competitive dailies during the same period. For selected years, these figures are: 1880, 239; 1920, 552; 1940, 181; and 1960, 61. The number of newspaper groups increased from 13 in the 1909–1910 period to 109 in 1960.[17]

Among reasons cited by Nixon and Ward for this decline in competition are the growth of an "objective" news style in wire service dispatches which reduces the differences between newspapers. In addition, an increase in importance of television news, preferences of advertisers for a single mass media outlet, and declining numbers of newspapers taken by suburban dwellers have worked toward reduction in competition. Hence, declining competition results from a combination of social and technological factors.

The *effects* of declining competition are not clear, nor is it clear just what anyone can, or should, do about it. Wilbur Schramm, one of the outstanding mass communications scholars of the century, views as essentially irreversible the economic trends bringing newspaper concentration:

> Concentration has come about because it fits better into the national economic system. For one thing, capabilities for serving large numbers of persons have immensely increased: fast presses, quick transportation, wire news connections to all the world, powerful broadcasting stations, cheap receiving sets, efficient means of duplicating films, and the growth everywhere of motion picture theaters. While these capabilities have grown, the cost of labor and equipment has also increased immensely, so that to provide a service to a small audience would be prohibitively expensive, and all the economics of the situation are in favor of large audiences.[18]

As newspapers became consolidated into ever larger units, libertarians decried the lessening of competing voices, different ideas. The Commission on Freedom of the Press concentrated particularly on this issue in its 1947 report, chiding newspapers to dig deeper, highlight significant issues, provide a meaningful opinion forum,

[17]Raymond B. Nixon and Jean Ward, "Trends in Newspaper Ownership and Inter-Media Competition," *Journalism Quarterly* 38 (Winter 1961), 3–14.
[18]Wilbur Schramm, *Responsibility in Mass Communication* (New York, 1957), p. 122.

and portray a representative picture of the constituent groups of a pluralistic society.[19]

Members of the press, in response, increasingly have adhered to what has been called the social responsibility theory of the press, the theory that the press has a special obligation to report all the news objectively (or at least fairly), a particularly important duty in the no-competition community.

As a result of economic centralizing forces shaped by technological advancement, enormous power has flowed into the hands of publishers. That these publishers (with some notable exceptions) have *consistently* used this power in a socially responsible way is not really clear. They *are* free from temptations to use "sensational" news (of the nineteenth-century type) and gimmicks of a competitive situation, yet have newspapers always been willing to probe deeply, stir up intrinsic economic interests when necessary, question foundations upon which a noncompetitive newspapers rests so safely? Is there, for example, any newspaper in America which would allow a columnist or editorialist *seriously* to explore alternatives to democracy/capitalism? How about communism? Yet John Stuart Mill pointed out that ideas need challenge to remain viable; this has never been more true of America than today.

Few places remain where one can compare competitive and noncompetitive newspapers. Perhaps consolidation is so fixed in the economic system (as Schramm implies) that these are moot questions. Although research by communications specialists shows some tendency for the competitive newspapers to devote less space to advertising and more to news, a more valid conclusion is that newspapers—subscribing to the same wire services and many of the same features and columnists—exhibit a distressing similarity. Typographically, they *are* different; typography unfortunately is skin deep.[20]

It is convenient (and cheap) to use wire copy. Wire service re-

[19]See Commission on Freedom of the Press, *A Free and Responsible Press* (Chicago, 1947).

[20]See for example Raymond B. Nixon and Robert L. Jones, "The Content of Non-Competitive Vs. Competitive Newspapers," *Journalism Quarterly* 33 (Summer 1956), 299–314; Gerard H. Borstel, "Ownership, Competition and Comment in 20 Small Dailies," *Journalism Quarterly* 33 (Spring 1956), 220–222; Wesley F. Willoughby, "Are Two Competing Dailies Necessarily Better Than One?" *Journalism Quarterly* 32 (Spring 1955), 197–204.

porters bring a competency and breadth to news coverage that most newspapers could not possibly duplicate. They bring the world, so to speak. It also is easy to allow wire news to fill up *too much* news space, to substitute for serious (and expensive) exploration of the local environment. The hard-pressed news editor often can do little else, as research clearly has indicated. The result for many is insulation from problems of the local community.[21]

THE CHALLENGE OF CONTROL

Without better understanding of the effects of mass communication on the patterns of social and political life, we face the prospect of a silent spring. We are not alone. The technologies which have pervaded the American experience have challenged the ability of our narrowly confined academic disciplines for dealing with the world in prospect. Yet mass communications scholarship must participate fully in the challenges of our age.

Mass communications scholars must seek continued and broadened studies of the effectiveness of mass communications on the full range of modern life. Many studies which fill research journals lack focus or clear meaning, a particular failing of some recent studies employing content analysis or historical method to study trivial problems. We more thoroughly need to know the relationship, for example, between crime reporting and free trial, conflict news and riot incitement, television viewing and its impact on social and family organization, government pressures and a free press. And we direly need more research aimed at establishing a *theoretical* framework for *general* understanding of mass communication processes. We need, in short, sounder understanding of the effectiveness of communication in order to understand how to act.

As communications scholars, we should attempt the direction and control of communication technology. We must not assume that progress necessarily implies improvement. One of the most disturbing aspects of McLuhan's excitement over cool media (which in his

[21]See for example Donald L. Shaw, "Surveillance vs. Constraint: Press Coverage of a Social Issue," *Journalism Quarterly* 46:4 (Winter 1969), 707–712; Wayne A. Danielson and John B. Adams, "Completeness of Press Coverage of the 1960 Campaign," *Journalism Quarterly* 38 (Autumn 1961), 441–452.

analysis reestablishes the old sensitivities and dignities of tribal life) is that he is, in effect, justifying "business as usual" in mass media development.

Meanwhile, we should promote establishment of local (and a prestigious national) press councils upon which men and women from all walks of life periodically can assess the performance of the press during particular times of crisis. In this regard, such journals as *Columbia Journalism Review* and *Nieman Reports* serve a particularly vital function in regularly focusing upon press performance. More frequently, communication scholars should regard the mass media as integrated into American economic and political life. Bryce W. Rucker brilliantly took this approach in *The First Freedom* (1968).

At least we are not powerless against expanding monopoly. As Rucker suggests, "If our laws can prevent railroads from owning steamship lines and aircraft manufacturers from owning more than small percentages of airlines, why can't we prevent newspaper-broadcasting-magazine-book publishing combines?"[22] Vice President Agnew drew a tirade of media criticism when he touched on this issue of media power and concentration in several 1969 speeches. Many questioned his motives, few his facts.

What of the future? Rucker quotes General David Sarnoff, board chairman of RCA, as visualizing simultaneous communication with the entire population of the earth via satellites which reflect broadcasts *directly* to FM radio and television receivers (no intermediating stations) and ultimately "total mass communications on a global scale," in other words, from New York to tribal villages. Somehow, given the limits of our present knowledge of mass communications, this is not comforting. It should not be.

[22]Bryce W. Rucker, *The First Freedom* (Carbondale, Ill., 1968), p. 222.

5 THE CHALLENGE OF REGIONALISM

Richard F. Hixson

Richard F. Hixson, Rutgers University, is the author of *Isaac Collins: A Quaker Printer in 18th Century America* and various scholarly articles.

There are about as many methods and approaches to history as there are historical periods or topics—or historians. Mine, which might be termed "regional biography," is really an outgrowth of the early "great man" writings.

Apparently, each subdiscipline writes its first histories in terms of great men. Certainly this happened in journalism, from Isaiah Thomas's, *The History of Printing in America* (1810; rev. ed., 1874) through Hudson, Lee, Payne, and culminating in Willard G.

Bleyer's, *Main Currents in the History of American Journalism* (1927). There has been more than a trace in later works, most notably in Kenneth Stewart and John Tebbel, *Makers of Modern Journalism* (1952).

At last, a handful of journalism historians are concentrating on figures less monumental, but perhaps as important as, Greeley and Hearst. We now have a biography of Ed Howe, the Kansas editor who may have influenced Midwestern thought more than William Allen White, and David Ross Locke ("Petroleum V. Nasby"), the Toledo editor who was an eloquent spokesman for the rights of man, has been given his due.[1] The list is growing, though slowly.

Other journalism historians, such as Professor Harold L. Nelson of the University of Wisconsin, are calling for a more disciplined approach to the subject, particularly an attempt to seek out the causes as well as the effect of major changes.[2]

Considering the importance of printers and publishers in our early history, it is surprising—and disappointing—that they have not received more attention from historians. Only Benjamin Franklin and Isaiah Thomas have received anything like adequate treatment.

When, a number of years ago, I began research on what was to be a long article on the establishment of the first regular newspaper in New Jersey, I had little notion that the project would become a book on printing and publishing in the Middle Atlantic region encompassing most of the eighteenth century.[3] Aside from a few imprint lists, only a small amount of interpretative research had been done on early regional press history.

A survey of the big histories of American press development convinced me that many of the accepted generalities were not applicable to New Jersey and the rest of the Middle Atlantic region. In fact, as I followed the movements of certain printers, it became apparent

[1]Calder M. Pickett, *Ed Howe: Country Town Philosopher* (Lawrence Kan., 1969), and John M. Harrison, *The Man Who Made Nasby, David Ross Locke* (Chapel Hill, N.C., 1969). For a discussion of American press historiography see Allan Nevins, "American Journalism and Its Historical Treatment," *Journalism Quarterly* 36:4 (Fall 1959), 411–422.

[2]Harold L. Nelson, "Guide to Morasses in Historical Research," *Journalism Educator* 19:1 (Spring 1964), 38–42.

[3]Richard F. Hixson, *Isaac Collins: A Quaker Printer in 18th Century America* (New Brunswick, N.J., 1968).

that, although printing shops operated in about the same way from town to town, colony to colony, and from region to region, the circumstances of their establishment, their *raison d'être*, were different.

Take, for example, the career of Isaac Collins, whose biography I ended up writing. Here is what I read in Mott's *American Journalism*: "Washington repeatedly encouraged the Patriot press; he aided in the establishment of the *New-Jersey Gazette* that his army might have a newspaper to read in the winter of 1777; he consigned quantities of wornout tenting to the papermills to be made into printing-paper. (p. 107)" And in Emery's *The Press and America*: ". . . it is interesting to note that Washington contributed his prestige to encourage the founding of the *New-Jersey Gazette,* which, for a time, served as a kind of army newspaper. (p. 121)"

That is the extent of references to the *Gazette* in the two most popular press history texts, a sin of omission, it seemed to me at the time, compounded by the fact that neither historian even mentions the name of Collins. But, lest my comments be interpreted as petty, academic criticism, I should point out that such neglect on the part of historians who write our sweeping general histories is more accurately the fault of regional and local researchers whose smaller works form the basis for eventual synthesis and generalization.

I will return to Collins's contributions as they feed my thesis on the need for more intense, detailed studies of early American press development. Another nagging example, meanwhile, is the London-born Philadelphia-New York printer William Bradford. The first printer in two colonies, his life as an honest tradesman in Philadelphia was made so uncomfortable (including a four-month confinement in jail during the great Quaker schism in the 1690s) that he moved on to New York City to resume his career and establish that city's first newspaper.

Bradford's story needs to be examined in detail because it is interwoven with the early conflicts between the printing press and the ruling order, in his case, Quaker political power in Philadelphia. Had Bradford refused to publish literature on both sides of the controversy, we might not be so obliged to want to know the full story; but he did not. The basic facts, according to Emery's *The Press and America,* are that, when Bradford balked at strong-arm tactics and would not refuse business from one faction, he was accused of seditious libel. His defense was that the jury must decide both the *law* and the *fact* of such cases, whereas heretofore it had been left to the judges to determine the point of law and to the jury to decide the authorship, or point of fact. Bradford prevailed, the jury could not agree, and he was released. Shortly afterwards he took his printing shop to New York. As Emery asserts, the issue that Bradford successfully raised in 1692 became a principal point in the case of John Peter Zenger some 40 years later.

The matter of press freedom is discussed elsewhere in this book, but I wish here to press the point for a continuing study of regional circumstances, such as the theocratic environment of the press in Massachusetts and Pennsylvania. A full study of Bradford, for instance, would lead the communications scholar into a search for printing bills still extant in local, state, and federal archives. Such research would increase our knowledge of official government printing as well as enlarge our comprehension of our social and economic past.

It was as editor of the *Gazette* that Collins probably exerted his greatest influence. Its meticulously edited and printed pages are an enduring source of information and pleasure. It was one of the best-looking papers of the time, and its editor was one of the staunchest defenders of freedom of the press in an era when publishing even the mildest paper was risky business. He saw himself as "a faithful guardian of the Liberty of the Press" and resisted several attempts to censor the *Gazette*.

Thanks largely to bibliographers, antiquarians, and typophiles we have a number of genealogical studies and imprint lists of colonial printers. Douglas C. McMurtrie has traced one of the most interesting phenomena of the early history of printing in the United States —the long line of printer-journalists in the Green family, starting with Samuel, the second printer in the English-speaking colonies.[4]

Samuel Green was printer to Harvard College for 40 years, during much of which time Harvard had the only press in town. One of his sons moved to Boston in 1681 to act as printer under Samuel Sewall and eventually to manage the press there until his death in 1690. Among his accomplishments was printing a broadside in 1689 which apparently was the first publication of foreign news in the colony. Wouldn't he be worth knowing more about? Or how about

[4]Douglas C. McMurtrie, "The Green Family of Printers," *Americana,* 1932.

his brother, Bartholemew Green II, who in 1704 became printer of John Campbell's *Boston News-Letter,* the first regular newspaper in America? For 40 years he was official printer to the governor and council of Massachusetts. Isaiah Thomas called him the "most distinguished printer of that period in the country." Samuel Green and his descendants formed a dynasty of printers that endured for five generations and included at least a score of colonial craftsmen; still, we know little about them.

We need to study representative persons who influenced social movements and technological developments. Of course, sufficient data must be available, but most scholars underestimate how much *is* available.

In writing the biography of Isaac Collins, I found out his career constituted an important part of the early history of printing, publishing, and journalism in the Middle Atlantic region. What started out as an article on the establishment of journalism in New Jersey ended as a book on regional history.

From his presses in Philadelphia, Burlington and Trenton, New Jersey, and New York City, in the years 1770 to 1808, came some of the finest specimens of American printing. He was foremost a book publisher and bookseller, but he also published a Revolutionary newspaper and served as New Jersey's official government printer.

I said earlier that the study covered most of the eighteenth century. By this I meant that as early as 14 years after his birth, he was indentured as an apprentice to the first printer in Delaware, another part of the Middle Atlantic region. Collins was born in 1746, indentured in 1760, a journeyman in 1767 in Philadelphia, and a master printer in 1770, owner of his own shop in New Jersey, where he worked until 1796 when he moved his equipment and family to New York City.

He issued many Quaker tracts and histories (he was a devout Friend), as well as numerous books about other faiths; however, he was equally well known as the publisher of outstanding works on slavery, education, American history, and medicine. His greatest single achievement as publisher and craftsman was his 1791 edition of the King James Bible, the second quarto edition to be printed in America.

As founding publisher and editor for more than eight years of the *New-Jersey Gazette,* New Jersey's first established newspaper,

Collins persisted in concepts of freedom of the press that sometimes conflicted with legislators and politicians. Although he lent his wholehearted support to the patriot cause during the Revolution, Collins was attacked by extremists who, in the words of Arthur M. Schlesinger, author of the magnificent *Prelude to Independence: The Newspaper War on Britain, 1764–1776* (1958), believed that "liberty of speech belonged solely to those who spoke the speech of liberty." Collins's position was simple: "My ear is open to every Man's Instruction but to no Man's influences."

In a 1969 article, Maurice R. Cullen, Jr., after a study of the colonial press, concluded that if the revolutionary experiment really was a class struggle, then the press must have played a minimal role.[5] One of the reasons he cites is the high illiteracy rate, and the "truth" of that rate has stirred journalism as well as other historians about as much as any topic one can suggest for this early period. Obviously, it is a vital question to ask.

Devout Quaker though he was, Collins held strong personal ideals of public justice and self-defense in wartime. The Society of Friends disowned him for nearly a decade on the grounds that his services as official printer to a revolutionary government and publisher of a patriot newspaper were tantamount to service in the militia. On the slavery issue, however, he had the full approval of his brethren, for he early freed his own slave and then helped in the movement to forbid slave-holding generally by welcoming manuscripts by reformers at a time when other printers did not.

Collins's place in the eighteenth century has been somewhat obscured by more vocal and more versatile contemporaries. Historians, like others, are attracted first to the spectacular and the unusual, but to understand the history of printing, publishing, and journalism in the United States, we must also study the lives and times of the people who set the early patterns and standards, men like Collins, William Bradford, James Franklin, and James Parker.

Craftsmen like Collins lived and worked during a pioneering period. Every innovation, however small, was to have a lasting influence. Collins also was an astute businessman at a time when few printers were. Toward the end of his career Collins owned two

[5]Maurice R. Cullen, Jr., "Middle-Class Democracy and the Press in Colonial America," *Journalism Quarterly* 46:3 (Autumn 1969), 531–535.

houses, one adjacent to his New York City shop and store and the other in the country. Collins was more affluent than most of his fellows, though perhaps more frugal. The fact that he conducted his business for nearly 40 years without interruption is a tribute to his business acumen. When he died, his estate was valued at nearly $36,000, a sizable sum in that day.

No printer in Collins's time became rich on his newspaper enterprise alone; in fact, the wealthy ones like Isaiah Thomas amassed their money by publishing and selling books. Collins, to his credit, sacrificed money and security during the years he edited and printed the *New-Jersey Gazette*. He started it with legislative support and money, but when the money ran out he carried it on against great odds for nearly nine years.

Printers were among the most respected members of their towns, not only because of their veiled "power of the press" but because they were interesting and knowledgeable persons—if once in a while a bit eccentric. Their shops were popular centers for talk and business.

Above all, Collins's life is an example, albeit small, of a "case" for studying a particular region's printing, publishing, and journalism. An apology may be in order, however, for drawing so heavily upon a personal experience; such work, whether by accident or by choice, would nonetheless enhance our more general understanding of American communications history. Two other obscure printers, John Dunlap and Eleazer Oswald of Philadelphia, have gotten consideration from Professor Dwight L. Teeter of the University of Wisconsin, particularly as their careers relate to government printing, press freedom, and political economy.[6] In the future, the big history books may be truly interpretative and integrated, less encyclopedic and chronological.

One outstanding contribution is Richard L. Merritt's *Symbols of American Community 1735–1775*. His content analysis of seven major colonial newspapers (four which tended to be conservative

[6]Dwight L. Teeter, "Press Freedom and the Public Printing: Pennsylvania, 1775–1783," *Journalism Quarterly* 45:3 (Autumn 1968), 445–451; and "John Dunlap: The Political Economy of a Printer's Success" (Paper presented to the Association for Education in Journalism, Berkeley, Calif., 1969). See also Peter J. Parker, "The Philadelphia Printer: A Study of an Eighteenth-Century Businessman," *Business History Review* 40:1 (Spring 1966), 24–46.

and pro-British and three which were less so) found that only the Virginia and Pennsylvania papers gave more prominence to British than to colonial events. There was, Merritt concluded, a common shift of attention toward the discussion of American news and problems in their columns.

Merritt found the *Pennsylvania Gazette* most preoccupied with European events, perhaps because of the colony's large German population, but perhaps also because for part of the period Benjamin Franklin was its editor. The *Virginia Gazette* was the laggard in terms of American news. "It would seem that, from the point of view of its communications and focus of attention, the Old Dominion retained closer ties to England throughout the last four decades of the colonial period than did the other provinces in America."[7] The *South-Carolina Gazette* was second only to the Massachusetts papers in space given to American symbols, which kept increasing over the last 14 years of the colonial era.

Another historian might adopt Merritt's technique to study the generally reluctant Williamsburg press. Until 1766, the Williamsburg press was entirely controlled by Royalist printers; despite their claims of nonpartisanship, they were reluctant to criticize the ruling government, which held the purse strings on public printing. A study of William Rind's career could clarify the history of another printing region.

In concluding a major part of the study, Merritt writes:

> If the middle colonies emphasized the other colonies as individuals and the southern colonies stressed the collective character of colonial society, Massachusetts was comparatively self-centered. It was not particularly prone to be attentive to other colonies, and was the least interested of the colonies in the collective concept. In a metaphorical sense, Massachusetts was an exporter of information that sought to rally the other colonies to its side in the struggle against colonial rule. By the last colonial decade at least, other colonies were quite likely to look to the Bay Colony as a primary source of news.[8]

It is interesting to note that of the seven colonial newspapers

[7]Richard L. Merritt, *Symbols of American Community 1735–1775* (1966), p. 73.
[8]*Ibid.*, p. 75.

Merritt selected as particularly important to study, only a couple have been written about by press historians; of the editors, only Franklin and Zenger have been treated adequately.

There are still plenty of worthy subjects awaiting the journalism historian, whether he is interested in individual printers, institutional histories of papers or printing firms, or social and economic movements.

For example, Rollo G. Silver, who has devoted many years to the study of early American printing, uncovered the career of Benjamin Edes, "a true Revolutionary patriot, who helped destroy the British power with his printing press." He was copublisher of the *Boston Gazette*.[9] How many others like him await discovery? Certainly we need a full study of Hugh Gaine, who lived long enough to be revered as the dean of American printers.

An excellent master's thesis at the University of Wisconsin by George E. Moranda, "The Financial Aspects of Benjamin Franklin's Printing House" (1964), showed, among other things, the attempts by Franklin to corner the newsprint supply of the nation. Another thesis at the same school, by Mary Ann Yodelis, "Economics and the Boston Newspapers 1763–1775" (1969) indicated that government printing was far less important to printers than most historians had thought.

Printers have always been a footloose breed. Just tracking them from place to place might give many clues about the spread of technology and typographical innovations. Granted, most of the early imprint checklists are incomplete, but there are more of these stuck away in file drawers on yellowing mimeographed paper than most researchers would assume. Finding them may be largely a matter of serendipity.

Lawrence C. Wroth's classic study, *The Colonial Printer* (1931; rev. ed., 1938), has much to commend it. It is a treasure trove on equipment and processes in colonial print shops. A more modest, but useful, contribution along the same line is "The Colonial Printer in Williamsburg," a pamphlet issued by Colonial Williamsburg, Inc., the same organization which distributes an excellent color movie by the same title.

[9]Rollo G. Silver, "Benjamin Edes, Trumpeter of Sedition," *Papers of the Bibliographical Society of America*, 1953.

And, of course, the advertisements in colonial newspapers are a never-ceasing source of wonder to the modern reader. Although many articles about such ads have bordered on the "gee-aren't-they-quaint" genre, Ronald Hoffman in 1969 showed the possibilities for such research. After a content analysis of the ads in eighteenth-century Maryland papers, he concluded that Maryland merchants really did not need the newspapers until at least 1790.[10] His study shows how regional and economic history can be joined.

Regional studies are the building blocks for general history. The more imaginative and sound they are, the better will be the general history books. The generalist must turn to them, both for their uniqueness and for the insights they offer in looking at broader areas.

[10]Ronald Hoffman, "The Press in Mercantile Maryland: A Question of Utility," *Journalism Quarterly* 46:3 (Autumn 1969), 536–544.

6 BLACK JOURNALISM: NEGLECTED NO LONGER

John D. Stevens

John D. Stevens, University of Michigan, is coeditor of this volume and author of its second chapter, which deals with freedom of expression. He teaches a graduate seminar in the black press.

Until the boom in black history in the late 1960s, blacks were as invisible in journalism history as in other history; they are still underrepresented. There is no comprehensive book on the modern black press, nor is there an adequate published biography of a black journalist. We have done better, but only slightly better, for the foreign-language press.

Academic interest in the black press was late in coming, although there were three early books. The classic work remains Frederick G. Detweiler, *The*

Negro Press in the United States (1922), but it is hardly a sound historiographic treatment. Even earlier were G. I. Penn, *The Afro-American Press and Its Editors* (1891), which has been reprinted and is available again, and Robert T. Kerlin, *The Voice of the Negro* (1919).

The lack of interest in the black press and black topics is indicated in back files of *Journalism Quarterly,* which until 1963 had published only two such articles (both by Professor Armistead Pride of Lincoln University). From 1963 through 1968, there were eight articles, and six more appeared in 1969; however, of the 14 recent articles, only two dealt specifically with the black newspaper press.[1]

The sudden deluge of books and articles on all phases of race relations (although relatively few directly on black journalism) threatened to immobilize the historian, but to the rescue came Professor Pride with his 1968 pamphlet, "The Black Press: A Bibliography." The work was the outgrowth of his lifelong interest in the black press and was supported by the Association for Education in Journalism (from which copies may be obtained by writing 425 Henry Mall, Madison, Wis. 53706). With this listing, journalism teachers and researchers had a key to the scattered literature. Truly, Armistead Pride ranks as the Frank Luther Mott of black journalism history.

Some 2700 black newspapers have been started in this country, of which about 200 survive. Of the present papers, all are weeklies except a few semiweeklies and two dailies (*Chicago Daily Defender* and *Atlanta World*). There is not an adequate published institutional study of *any* of them, nor of their editors.

Carter R. Bryan chronicled some aspects of early black journalism in a 1969 monograph.[2] His foreword begins:

> It is not the purpose of this monograph to serve as the final, definitive work on this long-neglected and scantily researched phase of history. Rather, it is the writer's hope that as a result of this brief survey other scholars will turn their attention to the

[1]George W. Bain, "How Negro Editors Viewed the New Deal," *Journalism Quarterly* 44:3 (Autumn, 1967), 552–54; Richard L. Beard and Cyril E. Zoerner II, "Associated Negro Press: Its Founding, Ascendency and Demise," *Journalism Quarterly* 46:1 (Spring 1969), 47–52.

[2]Carter R. Bryan, *Journalism Monograph* 12 (Association for Education in Journalism, 1969).

subject and that, consequently, lost newspapers and their forgotten editors who labored in the cause of freedom will be found
and restored to their rightful place in history.

What have the journalism history textbooks done with the black
press? Almost nothing. Frederic Hudson (like Willard Bleyer, James
Lee, John Tebbel, and Sidney Kobre later) simply ignored it. George
Payne acknowledged its existence, but called the first paper *Freeman's Journal,* instead of *Freedom's Journal*. Edwin Emery devoted
one paragraph, while Frank Luther Mott gave it nearly two (of his
900) pages.

Even *Columbia Journalism Review,* in many ways a bellwether
of trends in American journalism, largely ignored the black press
until 1970 when L. F. Palmer, Jr., did an excellent job of discussing
the relevancy (or lack of it) of the black papers to black readers.[3]
Palmer, now a reporter and a columnist for the *Chicago Daily News*
but formerly a staff member on two black papers, made it clear that
the days of national black papers were over and that many of the
local ones now are establishment-oriented. He also pointed out,
probably much to the amazement of many white readers, that by
far the largest circulation black paper in 1970 was *Muhammad
Speaks,* the voice of the Black Muslims, which circulated 400,000
or more copies each week. Second place was the *Baltimore Afro-
American* with 119,000, about the same as the unaudited estimated
circulation of the *Black Panther*. Only four other black papers had
circulations of more than 50,000.

One can no more ignore the religious press in studying black
journalism history than he can in studying the journalism of the
American colonies; religion is inexorably entwined with both.

Since the founding of the African Methodist Episcopal Church
in 1787, the black church has been a major force in the civil rights
struggle. Many black publications were sponsored by and devoted to
religious activities. Some of these journals were more militant on
racial issues than sectarian black papers dared to be. It is hard to
draw the line between religious and sectarian black papers, because,
like today's *Muhammad Speaks,* many have been both. Journalism
historians must remember that such journals are very much in the

Review 9:1 (Spring 1970), 31–36.
[3]L. F. Palmer, Jr., "The Black Press in Transition," *Columbia Journalism*

mainstream of black history. Somewhat the same can be said for journals published by predominantly black unions, such as A. Phillip Randolph's Brotherhood of Sleeping Car Porters.

The black press was founded in 1827 after an incident which Jerome Barron would label as a denial of access to the established media. When a black man sought first to place an article and then buy an ad on the slavery question in the *New York Sun* in 1827, he was told that "the *Sun* only shines on white men." He then went out and helped found *Freedom's Journal*.

An editorial in the first edition set the crusading spirit:

> In the spirit of candor and humility we intend by a simple representation of facts to lay our case before the public, with a view to arrest the progress of prejudice and to shield ourselves against the consequent evils . . . we must be firm and unwavering in our principles and persevering in our efforts.

Twenty years later, Frederick Douglass echoed the same spirit in his *North Star,* as has virtually every black journal since. NAACP Executive Secretary Roy Wilkins wrote: "Negro papers came into being as crusaders. And the minute they stop being crusaders and become chronicles, they're done."

Others see chronicling as the most important function for the black journals, which admittedly constitute a supplementary press. That is, black readers can and do obtain information about non-ethnic events from the white media, and they use the black media for more detail and additional insights into news of special interest. It is no secret that the white press has largely ignored the black community. The Kerner Commission was much more critical of the white media's day-to-day coverage of the ghetto than of their riot coverage. It was not many years ago that white newspapers refused to carry black obituaries or social news. The situation has changed less in that regard than many whites might realize.

American Press magazine surveyed its readers in 1968, and found that only 52 percent cover black social events, while 16 percent "seldom" do and 31 percent do not at all. Thirty-one percent still do not cover black engagements, and 55 percent run black obituaries "only when asked" or not at all. Slightly more than half (52 percent) carry features on black cultural events and only 45 percent on black celebrities, attitudes, and history. One-fourth still do not run photographs of blacks.[4] Remember: this survey was made in 1968.

The only black journalist to receive serious recent biographical treatment has been William Monroe Trotter, whose *Guardian* of Boston was an important force in the battle against the racial leadership of Booker T. Washington.[5] Others, notably Robert Lee Vann, have been the subject of unpublished theses and dissertations. The Vann thesis, completed in 1970 by Henry La Brie at Iowa, represents some of the finest traditions of journalism historical methods, particularly in the face of the dearth of available materials and the difficulty in obtaining answers to mail queries from often-overworked staff members on black papers. Certainly others deserve attention. Black newspapers invite family or dynasty treatments, since they tend to stay in the same families. This also explains why so many women have been prominent in black newspaper history, another worthy topic for investigation.

Black newspapers have employed white and oriental reporters, and many still do. No one has looked at this in any systematic way to see if it is merely "tokenism" in reverse, or whether some of these white reporters have risen to policy positions.

Perhaps the greatest need is for institutional studies of the black press. For example, while the *Chicago Defender* is often credited with promoting the migration of the rural blacks to the North during and after World War II, there is no serious study of this effort and its influence. The *Pittsburgh Courier* had the only American correspondent at the outbreak of the Italo-Ethiopian War, and so other American media obtained their news through him. Here is a good case study of a black reporter as a gatekeeper. How did his views influence American thinking on the conflict? William Worthy was an accredited correspondent for the *Baltimore Afro-American* when he challenged the travel ban on American newsmen both to Cuba and to Red China.

In many ways, World War II was the proudest moment for the black press which sent at least 30 correspondents into the war

[4]"Black Community in the News: Survey Results," *American Press* 86:9 (July 1968), 29.

[5]Stephen R. Fox, *The Guardian of Boston: William Monroe Trotter* (New York, 1970).

zones. The black papers devoted much money, time, and space to covering the war, largely in the (unfulfilled) hope that by proving his equality on the battlefield, the Black American would earn his equality at home. By contrast, the black papers were *not* staffing the Vietnam War. Why?

During both world wars, there were attempts to clamp special censorship restrictions on the black press. Among the publications which lost their second-class mailing permits under the Espionage Act in World War I was the NAACP's organ, *The Crisis.* The trouble arose when the magazine reprinted some correspondence from American officers to French commanders, suggesting the "dangers" of allowing the black doughboys too much social equality. The federal officials never claimed the correspondence was not genuine; they simply charged that it was "anti-war."

Sports news has formed the backbone of many black papers. Joe Louis was the champion of champions, but the black papers treated Cassius Clay/Muhammed Ali quite differently. In the days of all-black professional athletic teams, the papers were boosters, but the relationship between the teams and the papers has never been documented. How many people know that the *Pittsburgh Courier* paid Jackie Robinson's fare to attend tryout camps, first with the Boston Red Sox and then with the Brooklyn Dodgers? Certainly there are other aspects of sports coverage in the black press which should be examined.

During the 1930s and 1940s, newspapers were among the most successful of black businesses, rivaled only by insurance companies. Today, the *Courier* has only about one-third of its peak 1945 circulation, while others, such as the *New York Amsterdam News,* are more profitable than ever. Are there correlations between content and financial success in the black press? We really do not know whether there are for the white press.

Editor & Publisher International Yearbook listed 128 black papers in 1945, all but two of which had circulations of 10,000 or more and 16 of which had circulations over 40,000. In 1969, the same source listed 148 papers in 34 states and the District of Columbia, 24 of which had less than 10,000 circulation and only eight of which exceeded 40,000. Because of the ephemeral nature of small-circulation publications, the shift from large to small papers is probably even more pronounced than these figures would indicate.

Indices of sensationalism have been developed which could be applied to the content of black newspapers, especially over time, to see if they do thrive on sex and gore. Whitney Young of the Urban League suggested to a convention of white editors a few years ago that if the unpleasant content of black papers offended them, then they should work to make the black *communities* more pleasant places.

Black papers have been critical of coverage of the black community by white media; chronicling such criticisms would be a worthwhile project for some researcher. For example, the *Pittsburgh Courier* carried a long editorial on May 22, 1943, on racial identification in crime stories:

> A modern miracle was achieved last week when the world's leading daily newspaper, the *New York Times,* a pioneer in associating crime with colored people, carried a ten-inch news story on the murder of a colored navy chief by several "muggers" who were reported to police by colored residents—and all without using the word Negro. This is something new in American journalism, and having criticized the *New York Times* in the past for its policy in this connection, we hasten now to commend it and to express the hope that the rest of the American daily newspapers will follow its example.

The attitudes in the black press toward the use of the "colored," "Negro," "Afro-American," and "black" could also be traced and dated. As recently as World War II, the *Courier* felt compelled to insert dashes in "n————r" when its use was unavoidable in a direct quotation. These are the sorts of symbols which modern content analysis techniques can measure and analyze for clues to underlying and changing attitudes.

Other communications researchers have studied developing nations, and some of their findings could be applied to black America which in some ways resembles a developing nation. An ethnic underculture may be subject to some of the same forces which Daniel Lerner and others have observed abroad.

Beyond the work of Beard and Zoerner, there has been little research on cooperative efforts to gather and disseminate news and feature materials to black papers. This could include readyprint and syndicates, as well as the earlier equivalent—the scissors and pastepot.

Some black papers today carry without comment many syndicated columns, representing divergent views among blacks, in an attempt to be all things to all elements.

Emma Lou Thornbrough, a diligent student of the black press, has suggested that almost every successful black paper before World War I either had outright subsidies from political parties or indirect subsidies in the form of government printing contracts or political jobs for editors. Further, she suggests that Booker T. Washington kept black editors in line by channeling the relatively lucrative advertising from his Tuskeegee enterprises to "friendly" black papers.[6] The entire subject of subsidies to the black press is worth exploration.

What of their advertising support? Traditionally, it has come from small black-owned businesses; only recently have department stores and national advertisers become major supporters. No one has documented these changes or their implications. Classified ads are important in the black papers, too, both for the readers (in finding housing and special services) and as income for the papers.

What have been the experiences in attempting to unionize black newspapers? The *Amsterdam News* was believed to be the only black paper in the American Newspaper Guild in 1970, but how about the printing and mechanical trades, trades which include few blacks in their membership?

The black papers suggest endless content analyses, varying in sophistication from counting how many of them run editorials to symbol counts. A variety of studies suggest that only about half of American weeklies editorialize and that the percentage may be going down. Has the same thing happened in the black press?

Maxwell R. Brooks, in *The Negro Press Re-examined* (1959), counted references in five of the largest black papers to symbols which implied acceptance or rejection of American values. He found the black papers overwhelmingly accepted those values, but would the same be true today? Not only have attitudes and values changed since 1948 (the year which Brooks studied), but so have available research tools. For example, Richard B. Merritt was much more sophisticated in his analysis of colonial newspapers in *Symbols of American Community 1735–1775* (1966). His content analysis

[6]Emma Lou Thornbrough, "American Negro Newspapers, 1880–1914," *Business History Review* 40:4 (Winter 1966), 467–90.

suggested the growing estrangement of the colonies from England. Would similar techniques show the same sort of growing alienation in the black press of the 1960s?

Seminar students at the University of Michigan analyzed the content of 14 black newspapers during the first three months of 1970 and found that they stressed cooperation—both within the black community and between the races—much more than conflict. Of the space devoted to relational stories (those which recount contacts between individuals or groups), 60 percent went to cooperative stories. Most of the conflict was in crime and governmental news. The percentages were almost exactly reversed from a study done earlier of five metropolitan dailies which found 60 percent of such content devoted to conflict.[7]

The Watts riot of 1965, which awakened white America to the deep resentment in the black ghettos, provoked some studies and the inevitable symposia.[8] The solidest study was an interesting, but largely ignored, 49-page study of the role of the black media in the Watts riot, published by the School of Journalism of the University of Southern California.[9] After a detailed content analysis of two black weeklies and a black-oriented radio station during, before, and after the riot, the author concluded that the black media had done a responsible but ineffective job. They simply were drowned in messages from the daily newspapers and broadcasting stations. Such a study, limited as it is, offers suggestions for similar investigations into performance of black media in other crises.

One bonus of the new interest in the black American has been that many metropolitan newspapers published special series and supplements on black history, sometimes uncovering new information in the process—all grist for the historian's mill.

[7]John D. Stevens, "Conflict-Cooperation Content in 14 Black Newspapers," *Journalism Quarterly* 47:3 (Autumn 1970), 566–568: Edward R. Cony, "Conflict-Cooperation Content of Five American Dailies," *Journalism Quarterly* 30:1 (Winter 1953), 15–22.

[8]Proceedings of at least two were published. There are two articles on the black press in Paul L. Fisher and Ralph L. Lowenstein, eds., *Race and the News Media* (New York, 1967), but none on the ethnic press in Jack Lyle, ed., *The Black American and the Press* (Los Angeles, 1968).

[9]Frederic C. Coonradt, *The Negro News Media and the Los Angeles Riots* (Los Angeles, 1965). See also his, "A New Tone of Voice in the Negro Newspaper," *Grassroots Editor* 7:3 (July 1966), 17–18.

For black magazines, there is even less source material. In the standard one-volume history of magazines, Theodore Peterson's *Magazines in the Twentieth Century* (1964), there are about three paragraphs on black magazines, and Mott did not do much better, proportionally, in his five-volume, *A History of American Magazines* (1930–1969). The most scholarly treatment of black magazine history was in an Association for Education in Journalism convention paper in 1969 by Robert D. Bontrager.[10]

Bontrager makes it clear that there is more to the history of black magazines than the John H. Johnson empire, which after all, was begun only in 1942. *Mirror of Liberty* was the first magazine owned and edited by a black, and that was in 1837. Its stated interest was in "the moral, social, and political elevation of the free Afro-American in the North." The National Association for the Advancement of Colored People began publishing *The Crisis* in 1910, and its editors have included W. E. B. DuBois and Roy C. Wilkins. *The Crisis* back volumes have recently been reprinted and are available. The oldest scholarly journal devoted to black affairs is the *Journal of Negro History,* which began in 1916 and has carried many articles of importance for the journalism historian.

Johnson's magazines, especially *Ebony* with a circulation in excess of a million, do dominate the current scene. The only black-oriented publication with a larger circulation going into the 1970s was *Tuesday,* a monthly supplement inserted into metropolitan dailies. *Tuesday* was begun in 1965, and three years later, it had a circulation of 1.5 million.

An indication of changing attitudes appeared in the second edition of Roland E. Wolseley's, *Understanding Magazines.* Wolseley wrote:

> In recent years the author of this book has avoided, in the preceding edition and in university lectures, separating the periodicals issued for the Negro, black, or Afro-American citizens from those intended for people of white skin. But as the new edition was being prepared some black readers were asking for more direct and easily found attention to their culture, including their press.[11]

[10]The paper was based on his dissertation, "An Investigation of Black Press and the White Press Use Patterns in the Black Inner City of Syracuse, New York" (Syracuse University, 1969).

[11]Roland E. Wolseley, *Understanding Magazines,* 2nd. ed. (Ames, Iowa, 1969), p. i.

The Syracuse University journalism professor estimated there were 100 such magazines which "perhaps, as the Negro people attain-first-class citizenship, will become economically more secure and influential."

The trend toward specialization of magazine markets was nowhere more apparent as the 1970s began than in the black magazines. Earlier magazines had been specialized enough simply because they were aimed at the black population; the new entries concentrated on sections of that market. For example, *Essence* and *Sophisticated Lady* were aimed at fashion-conscious black women. Both were beautiful monthlies, the former produced under the watchful eye of Gordon Parks. *Black Enterprise,* which made its debut in August 1970, had a controlled circulation of 100,000 black business and professional men, elected officials, students, and heads of trade and fraternal groups. Another 60,000 copies were distributed by major corporations. All three started with adequate capital in the bank and with solid advance sales of advertising; they were anything but fly-by-night operations.

Where are the studies of the black magazines and their editors and publishers? There is not even an adequate treatment of John H. Johnson.

In its death throes, network radio discovered the black audience, but it discovered it too late. *Ebony* had shown by 1950 that there was an audience of blacks worth the attention of national advertisers. ABC put Jackie Robinson on as narrator of a series, but no sponsors appeared, and the show was dropped. CBS had the same experience when it tried a show featuring Mahalia Jackson.

When the NAACP protested at its 1951 convention about the stereotyping on "Amos 'n' Andy," much of the white nation was honestly shocked. They had never thought of their all-time favorite radio comedy show as derogatory. About the same time, "Amos 'n' Andy" was transferred to television, but with an all-black cast. Suddenly the stereotyping which had been implicit on radio became painfully explicit. The show died and a few years later was withdrawn even from overseas reruns.

As radio went local, station after station either added black programming or at least a black disc jockey. WERD of Atlanta became the first black-owned station in 1951; it was sold 17 years later to whites, but it continued its black programming.

The spread of black programming and black ownership needs careful documentation by journalism historians.[12] Individual station histories, especially for WERD, cry for attention.

In 1970, soul radio was a $40 million-a-year business, with 116 stations programming exclusively for blacks and another 300 part-time. Of the 13 black-owned stations, six were owned by two "chains": singer James Brown owned AM stations in Knoxville, Augusta, and Baltimore, while Bell Broadcasting owned AM and FM stations in Detroit and an AM in St. Louis. Is the programming of black-owned stations significantly different from white-owned stations beaming to blacks? We have no studies to show whether it is.

While there still were no black-owned television stations in 1970, black action groups have become active in challenging renewal of licenses of stations which they believe ignore the black segment of their audiences. In some cases, such as the challenge to a Jackson, Mississippi, station, the leadership was provided by white church groups; in others, local black groups carried the ball. It is a development worth chronicling.

Another phenomenon is the recurring hoaxes which have played an interesting, if minor, role in American journalism history. These range from fabricated articles in colonial newspapers (often signed with a nom de plume) to the war of the worlds in the Yellow Press to the wide circulation of an editorial in 1969, allegedly from the *Chicago Tribune,* which opposed further school integration. That people believe the hoaxes tells us something about their predisposition, as well as their gullibility. One would be hard-pressed to find a better example than the phony pamphlet used heavily in the 1864 campaign by the Democrats to embarrass the Abolitionist Republicans. The pamphlet, supposedly written by a black woman, argued that since Americans owed their power to a mixture of the races, what was needed was wide-scale mixed marriages. It struck a deep antiblack chord in the North, and the outrageous proposition was debated in drawing rooms, in learned societies, and even in Congress. It was not until after the election that the true authors, two staff writers on the *New York World,* unmasked themselves. The public had been fed for so long on "proofs" of black inferiority that they

[12]An example is Clotye M. Murdock, "Negro Radio Broadcasting in the United States" (M.A. thesis, University of Wisconsin, 1960).

received the account of black superiority with the same gravity, the same naïveté.[13] Have we really advanced much further in the ensuing century?

If anything, the need for education in these matters is greater today than ever. One of the problems for the teacher of journalism history is whether to teach a separate course on black journalism or to integrate it into existing courses and seminars. A panel at the 1969 convention of the Association for Education in Journalism concluded that the first priority was to redesign present courses and to add new ones as soon as possible.[14]

What is the historic role of the black press, and has that role changed today? Black leaders and black editors often point out that the first black newspaper in 1827 was an organ of protest against slavery and that the black press has been a protest organ ever since. They will cite the (losing) battles to prevent the reestablishment of segregationist governments and institutions in the South following Reconstruction, the battle against Jim Crow laws from the Progressive Era on, the opposition to discrimination against black servicemen and defense workers in World War II, and the unflagging support of the NAACP's legal battles for equality in the 1940s and 1950s. But their recitation often stops there.

Black newspaper editors became "recognized black leaders" during and after World War II. They were invited to White House conferences, flattered by government officials, and occasionally rewarded with political patronage. They were voices of moderation and reason, but many of these editors were unprepared for the abrupt change in tactics in the civil rights struggle which began with the sit-ins in 1960. This tactic may have been nonviolent, but it was not dignified, either. There is no published study of the content of black newspapers during this pivotal period, a period which inescapably was an identity crisis for the black newspapers as well as the black population.

Many of these papers apparently still have not resolved the dilemma. On one hand, they certainly do not want to lose their tra-

[13]J. M. Bloch, *Miscegenation, Melaleukation, and Mr. Lincoln's Dog* (New York, 1958).

[14]Tape available for loan from AEJ Executive Secretary, 425 Henry Mall, University of Wisconsin, Madison 53706.

ditional readership—the older, middle-class black who is committed to integration. Not only are there many of these readers, but the potential advertising from the black businesses comes from this sector. On the other hand, they must try to attract younger, more militant readers. There is more than chronological age at work here, too, since many older blacks are more disillusioned and radical than they once were. There is an added problem to the papers in becoming too moderate, and that is attracting young black staff members. This problem is serious enough because of the many jobs available on white media for black journalists; it becomes even more serious if the black newspapers do not offer some feeling of relevancy to a potential employee, a reward which some might choose over the higher salaries on white media.

No one has published a study of the employment problems of the black papers, including such questions as mobility of staff members within the paper, their movement to other black and to white media, their age, their personal philosophies, their salaries. There have been studies of professionalization among daily newspapermen and among broadcasters; a parallel study of newsmen in black media would be most welcome.

What is the future of the black press? It was not too many years ago that even the black editors thought they would work themselves out of a job. Once the nation was integrated and largely color-blind, then they believed there would be no need for a black press. Events of the 1960s dimmed this prospect, and the new black pride assured the need for a separate press. Some observers, of course, never had expected anything else. For example, as Gunnar Myrdal wrote in his classic *An American Dilemma:*

> No feasible widening of the reporting of Negro activities in the white press will substitute for the Negro press. What happens to Negroes will continue to have a relatively low "news value" to white people, and even the most well-meaning editor will have to stop far short of what Negroes demand if he wants to satisfy his white public.[15]

Certainly there are no signs of the imminent death of the black press as the 1970s begin; but there are signs that the older "estab-

[15]Gunnar Myrdal, *An American Dilemma* (New York, 1944), p. 924.

lishment" papers might be in for severe challenges. In Milwaukee, Detroit, St. Louis, and elsewhere, there were new, more militant black papers hurling down the gauntlet. For the black press, as for the white, offset lithography and other technological advances lowered the entrance fee to the publishing business. No longer did a potential publisher have to invest in expensive printing equipment; he could job it out, and that is what the new breed of black papers is doing.

Black journalism apparently is entering a new phase, one which looks to be at least as interesting and exciting as its earlier phases. Perhaps this time, the journalism historian will be alert enough to study the developments and to gather source materials for the journalism historian of the future.

7

THE JOURNALIST AS SOCIAL CRITIC

John M. Harrison

John M. Harrison, of Pennsylvania State University, is author of *The Man Who Made Nasby* and many articles. He is a former Nieman Fellow at Harvard, and in 1970 organized and cochaired a national symposium on muckraking.

An ignorant and bigoted village "bummer" . . . . a fey and ironic Irish saloonkeeper . . . . a cockroach with literary ambitions. . . . This is a strange trio to cite as representative of what is best in the tradition of the press as social critic in America. Yet not so strange, perhaps, in light of the fact that it was the fool, the jester in cap and bells, who served for so many centuries as conscience of the court in those kingdoms whose bolder spirits explored the North American continent and established here a new nation—one in which a high priority was assigned to free and open expression.

Today their names are almost forgotten. Who has so much as heard of Petroleum Vesuvius Nasby? A few, perhaps, may recall one of Martin Dooley's aphorisms ("the Supreme Court follows the illiction retoorns," for example) which editorial writers and television commentators sometimes cite in relation of today's problems. In the case of Archy the cockroach, some may even have sampled one of the anthologies which actually remain in print of his adventures, and those of Mehitabel, the amorous and amoral cat. Yet none of the three would be recognized by more than a handful of viewers if their names were flashed on a television screen, though each was a lively and influential contributor to American journalism within the last hundred years.

These were not, of course, the real names of the men who used them in the columns of the newspapers for which they wrote. Petroleum V. Nasby was the pseudonym of David Ross Locke (1833–1888), Mr. Dooley that of Finley Peter Dunne (1867–1936), and Archy was the creation of Don Marquis (1878–1937). But, with the possible exception of Marquis, none of the three would be known at all today were it not for the fictitious character he devised to serve his journalistic purposes. Each had some measure of literary talent, and each experimented with other forms of writing. But it was as humorist and satirist, and as practicing journalist, that each achieved the fame he deserved—fleeting though it may have been.

They are representative of a long and honored tradition. American journalists were not the first writers to have chosen humor and satire as their weapons. These have been favorites of the social critic, who has found them useful and effective for a number of reasons, over a period of many centuries. From Juvenal to Addison and Steele, the satirist has aimed his sharpest barbs at the society of which he was a part, couching them in inverted forms which served the utilitarian purpose of putting their authors safely beyond the reach of the censor.

The First Amendment to the Constitution of the United States undoubtedly minimized the need for this protection which the satirist's weaponry traditionally afforded him. Yet those Americans who have taken it up have found satire's inversion and indirect attack equally effective in their role as critics. Satire, in fact, may have been peculiarly suited to the needs and purposes of American journalists. Its reliance on exaggeration meshed well with the tall-tale humor that was characteristic of the young nation. The social critic found it easy to attack his targets by blowing them up to larger-than-life-size figures which extended a familiar tradition into a new dimension.

How much of American humor and satire first appeared in the pages of newspapers is remarkable in itself. Norris W. Yates points out, for example, that of the 16 writers he studied in *The American Humorist: Conscience of the Twentieth Century*, "all but one were journalists by profession."[1] Indeed, almost all of this country's great humorists and satirists began their careers as staff members of, or contributors to, the thousands of newspapers that sprang up in the United States during the nineteenth century.

These men have been poorly served by historians generally. Where literary history is concerned, there is little room to complain. Of their number, only Mark Twain achieved real literary distinction. But these were journalists—even Twain at the beginning—who wrote for tomorrow's newspaper. The very materials they used were necessarily so topical that much of what they wrote had lost its impact, along with its meaning, in a few months or years. Their grotesqueries of style, often an important element in their appeal to their contemporaries, soon went out of fashion and reading them today may require almost as much effort as translating from another language.

Political historians seem to have thought little of their importance, seldom recognizing their impact on the events of their times beyond an obscure footnote, perhaps citing the ubiquitous statement of George S. Boutwell attributing the Union victory in the Civil War to "the Army, the Navy, and the Nasby letters." But political historians are notoriously afflicted with myopic vision, which seldom permits them to see beyond what is going on at the center of the stage. As for their colleagues whose concern is with social and intellectual history, their eyes are only for the major figures and forces of whatever period occupies their scholarly attention.

It is to the historians of journalism, then, that one might expect to turn for a searching examination of the significance of these humorists and satirists who wrote for the popular newspapers and

[1]Norris W. Yates, *The American Humorist: Conscience of the Twentieth Century* (Ames, Iowa, 1964), pp. 351–352.

magazines of their times. Yet a careful reading of representative histories of American journalism suggests that they have not done so. In fixing their attention on the Days, the Bennetts, the Greeleys, the Hearsts, and the Pulitzers, they have ignored the men whose writings constitute the most effective social criticism contributed by journalists. When they are mentioned at all, these men usually are discussed as some sort of side-show oddity—as representative of "features" in one instance, of "the colyum" in another. Thus, their significance as social critics has been almost entirely lost, which is not so much a personal tragedy as a minimizing of the part the press has played in social criticism.

Any attempt to survey the role of the humorist and satirist as social critic in the American press, from its beginnings to the present, would obviously require an entire volume. So it is necessary to choose representative figures, through whom it may be possible to observe in microcosm the functioning of the journalist as social critic. Any number of writers might have been selected for this purpose, and Locke, Dunne, and Marquis would not be universal choices as the best and most significant satirists produced by American journalism. They are chosen, in part, because they represent three periods when newspapers and magazines have functioned most effectively in the role of social critic. These are:

1. The Civil War and Reconstruction (1860–1875),
2. The Progressive Era (1890–1910), and
3. The Interim Between World Wars (1918–1940).

Each period is notable for the number of writers who turned their talents to satire and who, in varying degree, played a significant role in directing public attention to the problems of the contemporary society. These were times when the United States faced a crisis of conscience, times when the conflict of ideas that is presumably so important an element of democratic government was a reality, not just a theoretical concept. They were periods in which the social critic was most needed in the land.

If the principles of representative democracy were to be sustained, it was essential in each instance that this social criticism should reach the widest possible audience—not just an intellectual or social or economic elite, but great numbers of people. Thus, it was to the newspapers—and, in some instances, the popular magazines—that the public must be able to look for the kind of meaningful commentary that would offer analysis of these crises and point the way to solutions.

Clearly, this function of newspapers and pamphlets was in the minds of the men who wrote the Bill of Rights when they began to have second thoughts about what must be stipulated—not assumed—in making the Constitution a meaningful document. What the First Amendment sought to achieve was a guarantee of the right of free expression, the right to criticize, to take the unpopular—even heretical—position. So its authors declared that "Congress shall make no law respecting an establishment of religion, or prohibiting the free exercise thereof; or abridging the freedom of speech or of the press. . . ."

All these are matters of conscience and they are joined meaningfully, not haphazardly, in this single article. The men who wrote it obviously sought to establish the unrestricted exercise of the critical function, which is always the first casualty of any attempt to impose official repression.

It is necessary to look only at the role of pamphlets and newspapers in the last years of the Colonial period to appreciate why Thomas Jefferson, James Madison, and others were so concerned to establish complete protection of the right to criticize. They had seen and known what happened to those who had dared to be critical. Whether it was John Peter Zenger in prison because he printed material that displeased a colonial governor, or Thomas Paine hounded by the authorities of three nations for his assaults on established concepts of government and religion, it was the critic who had suffered the harshest repression. They wanted to establish the right to criticize beyond the reach of any who might seek to abridge it.

On the whole, it seems likely that the men who wrote the Bill of Rights would be disappointed that the press in the United States has made such sparing use of the function of social critic. Looking back over a period of almost 200 intervening years, one is struck by the fact that as newspapers have grown in numbers and in potential as social instruments, their influence in this direction has steadily declined. There are several "golden ages" in which the press has seized the challenge, always present, to provide meaningful and influential criticism of the American society. But it has not managed to sustain this function. Perhaps the reasons for this failure can be ascertained through observing the work of some journalists who have fulfilled this essential role as social critics.

.   .   .

There are more differences than similarities among the lives and works of David Ross Locke, Finley Peter Dunne, and Don Marquis. Locke and Marquis came from similar backgrounds—both were poor boys with relatively little formal education, the products of small towns toward which they displayed a not uncommon mixture of nostalgia and contempt. Both went to work before completing high school and there was more of necessity than of choice in their becoming journalists. Dunne, on the other hand, was a native of metropolitan Chicago, the son of moderately wealthy parents, who obtained his high school degree and might certainly have gone on to college had he not preferred a career in newspapers.

What they had in common, of course, was an interest in journalism, a perception of the problems that were crucial in their respective times, and a flair for satire which each used to make meaningful and influential comment on those problems. Even in this area of common interest and methods, however, the three used their talents in widely varying ways.

David Ross Locke was a big, bluff man, coarse in appearance and manner, though not insensitive. His weapon was the shillelagh and he wielded it with free-swinging gusto. Instinctively, his target was the jugular and he went for it unerringly and with devastating effectiveness. He lived in violent times and his was a violent kind of satire—bitter, brutal, with no holds barred.

Petroleum Vesuvius Nasby, who was the principal agent of Locke's bludgeoning commentary, came straight out of the American tradition of the backwoodsman. He was a thoroughly despicable character—a coward, a braggart, mean, bigoted, self-serving. His ignorance was magnified by the atrocious spelling Locke employed in all the Nasby letters. He was lazy, vicious, crude. Locke made him deliberately so, of course, to represent all that was worst in the men who sought to undermine the Union cause, and were variously known as

Copperheads and Butternuts. Distorted and magnified though the image was, Nasby represented those of Locke's Ohio neighbors—whose counterparts were to be found throughout the North—whom he regarded as the most dangerous threat to the values he held to be of greatest importance.

Nasby was the perfect vehicle for Locke's comments; few satirists have matched their principal weapon so well to the temper of the times. In the midst of fratricidal war, and in the bitterness of the troubled period of attempted reconstruction that followed it, there was no place for the niceties of polished wit. Locke was an early practitioner of overkill, and he scored repeated and devastating hits on his targets with these Nasbian blockbusters.

Critics were subsequently to minimize Locke's satire as gross and heavy-handed. He was "unfair," they alleged, to the South and to those in the North who took a position other than his in relation to the war and its aftermath. But of course he was unfair, which was exactly his purpose and the reason why the Nasby letters were so effective among his contemporaries. The whole secret of his success lay in his skill in gauging the nature of his audience and the passions that motivated it.

Finley Peter Dunne was a very different sort from Locke. Growing up in Chicago, he early became associated with other young writers and artists who were members of the Whitechapel Club, where he was exposed to the radicalism of the Populist era. Politically and socially, he was much more sophisticated than Locke, and these differences are apparent in what he wrote as Mr. Dooley. Dunne introduced Martin Dooley to the readers of Chicago newspapers in the last decade of the nineteenth century and, though the peak of his career is separated from Locke's by no more than 25 years, profound changes had taken place in the prevailing intellectual and emotional atmosphere. Dunne is closely associated with the Progressive Era in American politics—a time in which the first genuinely concerted attack on long accepted values and institutions was launched, in large part by that group and journalists whom Theodore Roosevelt was subsequently to label "muckrakers." It was a time, too, when great reliance was placed on the ability of the electorate—through popular reforms in the political system—to achieve significant changes in the whole of American society.

Many of the muckrakers and the leading political figures in the Progressive movement were close friends and associates of Dunne, who shared their concern with the need to effect institutional and societal change. Two things Dunne did not share with them, however—the doctrinaire concept of the infinite perfectibility of man and their sober humorlessness. Dunne capitalized on these differences in the guise of Martin Dooley, who managed simultaneously to attack the targets at which the muckrakers took aim and to poke fun at the reformers who sought to make over the whole system of American values, albeit within the framework of the democratic political system.

Mr. Dooley, the unschooled but wise Irish barkeep, performed as social critic in the most complete meaning of the term. His was a satire far different from David Ross Locke's faintly ironic, mildly amusing, always reflecting Dunne's Progressive convictions, yet ever wary of the pitfalls that awaited the reformer who placed too much faith in his political panaceas. Mr. Dooley once commented on President Theodore Roosevelt's appointment of a commission to study the causes of unhappiness among American farmers. He speculated that if such a commission were ever named to investigate the causes of Martin Dooley's unhappiness, he would suggest these possible improvements in his lot:

> I wud like a little more loose change in th' till. I prefer to be a year or two younger, an' to be able to sleep an hour or two longer in th' mornings. An Act iv Congress curin' th' pain in me back or causin' a few tufts iv hair (wavy brown preferred) to grow on th' top iv me head wud be much appreciated. An appropriation f'r a new stovepipe hat f'r St. Pathrick's Day wud be as balm to me ag-nized spirits. I have two or three acquaintances I wud like to have bastinadoed. But beyond these simple wants there is nawthin' I cud ask the commission to do f'r me, an' they'd pay no attention to thim. They'd probably repoort that th' plumbin' in me house was defictive an' that th' roof needed mending, as if ayther iv thim things caused lines in me face.[2]

This catalogue of blessings to be petitioned for, but scarcely ex-

[2]Finley Peter Dunne, *On Making a Will and Other Necessary Evils,* pp. 21–22.

pected, may be as indicative of the substance of Finley Peter Dunne's Progressivism as any definition that could be formulated. It contained none of the dogmatism that characterized the attitudes of so many of his contemporaries. Yet the evidence suggests that he was as effective as any writer of his time in keeping before the public those issues and questions that were central to the Progressive movement.

Don Marquis, who was born ten years after Dunne, began his career in journalism relatively late in life. For the better part of ten years, after leaving Walnut, Illinois, where he was born and grew up, Marquis had been a roamer, working at an assortment of jobs, including a brief tour with a theatrical company. He was almost 30 years old when Joel Chandler Harris hired him in 1907 as an assistant editor of the *Uncle Remus Magazine* in Atlanta. Harris died the year after Marquis began work for him and his magazine suspended publication a few months later. Marquis moved from Atlanta to New York where, in 1912, he began writing a daily column, "The Sun Dial," for the *Sun*. It was here that Archy, the "literary cockroach," made his first appearance.

Don Marquis's purposes in creating Archy obviously were different from those of David Ross Locke and Finley Peter Dunne, who used Nasby and Dooley from the outset to carry on campaigns by satire which were intended to serve specific political ends. Archy—along with his constant companion, Mehitabel—was a creature of Marquis's whimsy, intended to amuse readers of "The Sun Dial" and to help fill that yawning chasm of space every day. Yet Marquis soon realized that he had in Archy a most effective and convenient means of voicing social criticism. That it was light-hearted in tone, that it came from the typewriter of a lowly insect, made it more palatable to his readers, and thus more effective in puncturing the illusions and frauds at which he directed his barbs.

Archy was—as Nasby and Dooley had been before him—the ideal spokesman for his times. This was the period immediately following the World War I in which the pretensions and excesses that were its surface manifestations were being attacked by those who saw through its shams and deceits. In American humor and satire, this was the age of the "little man"—confused, uncertain, a victim of all the forces of his environment that were destroying the individual, reducing him to the role of futile pawn. Archy was the littlest of these helpless victims, the most despised and insignificant of insects caught in the grip of circumstances in which his very existence was constantly threatened. The irony of his railing against the inexorable forces he opposed was greatly magnified by his very insignificance.

Marquis is closely identified in the public mind with the 1920s, though in fact he quit writing for newspapers in 1924, when he retired from the *Herald Tribune,* to which he had moved from the *Sun* two and one-half years earlier to write a column called "The Lantern." He turned then to writing plays and fiction, and his literary talents were considerable, if not of the first rank. But the link between him and the twenties is a logical and proper one. Archy and Mehitabel, indeed, may be said to represent the very characteristics most closely associated with that colorful decade. Both were hedonists, though Mehitabel's hedonism was a religion while Archy entertained grave doubts about his way of life. They provide an interesting and representative contrast in prevailing attitudes toward the "new morals" which were the object of a fixation of the time and toward which Marquis obviously had ambivalent feelings. They are skeptical, even cynical, but theirs is a gentle kind of cynicism, with more amusement than contempt in it.

As a satirist and social critic, Don Marquis has had few equals among American journalists. There was a bite to his writings, yet there was little bitterness. Among his contemporaries, he stands somewhere between H. L. Mencken and Ring Lardner, on the one hand, Robert Benchley and James Thurber, on the other. In relation to David Ross Locke and Finley Peter Dunne, he is much closer to the creator of Mr. Dooley than to the man who made Nasby. Yet it should be emphasized again that a part of the effectiveness of each was the degree to which he was attuned to the temper of his times.

•   •   •

The impact of each of these three journalists extended far beyond the readers of the newspapers for which they wrote. In their respective times, Locke's Nasby, Dunne's Dooley, and Marquis's Archy were more widely known than all but a handful of the public figures of the day, and each came to be regarded by those who read them as flesh-and-blood persons. The collected writings of all three circulated widely throughout the country. In the case of both Locke and Marquis, there was at least some measure of resentment that the make-believe characters they had created seemed likely to become the one thing for which each would be remembered.

Journalism at its best, of course, does reach out beyond the limitations of those who write it and those for whom it was ostensibly written. This is seldom true of the accounts of current events that comprise the bulk of newspaper content, though occasionally there is reporting of such quality that it survives the event it describes. Nor is it true of much of the straightforward commentary of the daily editorial columnist, which has little of either style or timelessness to preserve it beyond the moment of publication.

One turns, then, to the social critic who has something to say about the substantial problems of his times and says it in such a way that it commands attention beyond the audience to which it is immediately addressed. This is, surely, an important part of what the framers of the First Amendment envisioned when they insisted that freedom of expression must be unrestricted by governmental decree. Why, then, has there been so little of it? And why, as the mass media have expanded in scope and pervasiveness, has the proportionate amount of meaningful social criticism declined?

As much as anything, no doubt, the very nature of popular journalism is responsible for this state of affairs. Once the economic base of the media had been broadened—first in number of readers, then in volume of advertising—certain limiting influences began to operate. For now the reaction of the individual reader to what he read became a matter of primary concern, and the fear of offending any considerable number of these individuals became an even greater factor. Newspapers and popular magazines might take a position on political issues, though even here there was danger of economic sanctions that could be costly to those media which espoused views unpopular among its readers and advertisers. Where the great social issues were concerned, the threat of retaliation was so ominous that only the bravest—or richest—of editors and publishers dared speak out against accepted values.

It was these circumstances, beyond doubt, that led to the expression of so much of the social criticism that has appeared in the popular media in the form of satire. The First Amendment did not, as things worked out, provide the measure of protection for free expression of ideas which those who wrote it had imagined it would. Just as in the times when monarchs and their vengeful agents had

restricted the speech and writings of social critics, the very demo-
cratization of the press in the United States created conditions which
made it difficult to express forthrightly those ideas that were regarded as heretical, or even unpopular.

So it was, again, that satire became the most effective means of
giving voice to critical comment. What could not be said forthrightly in the name of the newspaper and its editor became somehow
acceptable when it was represented as the opinion of a village
"bummer," an Irish saloonkeeper, or a cockroach with literary ambitions. Even the bluntness of Petroleum V. Nasby drew a large audience, and it was possible for David Ross Locke, as Nasby, to indulge
in the most savage attacks on the Copperheads or on President
Andrew Johnson and those who supported his position in the fight
on Reconstruction policies. As for Finley Peter Dunne, employed by
a publisher who was deeply in debt, it was only through Martin
Dooley that he could have taken a position in support of the Pull-
man strike, which was strongly opposed by the very men to whom
his publisher was indebted.

In the eight decades between 1860 and 1940, the satirist often
served as the conscience of the press in America. His barbed comments were among the most widely read and popular features of the
nation's newspapers and magazines. He might question the most
sacred values in a society that was, for long periods of time, caught
up in material considerations and conspicuous consumption. His
readers laughed with him and then began to question the very
values he lampooned. The satirist of this period was the court
jester, the town fool, using his cap and bells to mask and soften the
cutting edge of his criticism, while scoring repeatedly on his targets.

To some of his more earnest contemporaries, those who failed to
appreciate the effectiveness of what he wrote, he sometimes seemed
trivial. Finley Peter Dunne, for example, was derided by Francis
Hackett for concentrating on the patent trivialities and jocularities
of the paper-made American world. Hackett conceded that he
scores hard and often—on a newspaper target, but deplored the fact
that "only occasionally does he disregard that target and pierce the
heart of life."[3] What Hackett failed to see, of course, was that
Dunne took deliberate aim on his "newspaper target" and, in doing

[3]Francis Hackett, *New Republic*, September 24, 1919.

so, was at least as effective as those of his contemporaries who believed they alone were able to "pierce the heart of life." Dunne, like Locke and Marquis, offered social criticism that reached millions of Americans precisely because it exploited the potential of the popular media.

      •   •   •

Humor and satire in American journalism reached their peak in the decade of the 1920s. Many of the writers who helped achieve this high point carried on into the 1930s, though with somewhat lessened impact because the Great Depression made their weapons seem inappropriate to many. There were fewer icons to smash, fewer pretensions to puncture, in a time when many Americans lived in actual want and others teetered precariously on its brink. Almost everyone asked questions now about nearly all the social, political, and economic values of the society. In these circumstances, the court jester no longer needed to ask them. Had he sought to treat these matters in his usual light-hearted fashion, the public's reception of his foolery would surely have been hostile.

But the continuing decline of humor and satire in the popular media during the 30 years since the onset of World War II has been the subject of much speculation and controversy. Why, in the decades of the 1950s and the 1960s, has there been no resurgence of the sort of social criticism that was so plentiful, and so effective, in that earlier postwar era? The times seemed to have been made for a Don Marquis, a Ring Lardner, or an H. L. Mencken, who might puncture the pretensions of an increasingly affluent, smug, and pompous society. What an inviting target for the satirist's barbed shafts was presented by a mushrooming federal establishment that seemed more and more to assume a divine right to manage not just the affairs of the American people, but those of all the world.

There were a few—a very few—manifestations of lively and trenchant satire in the media. Notable among these were not the writers for newspapers and magazines, but those who created cartoons and comic strips—Al Capp, Walt Kelly, and Charles Schulz. Capp's "Li'l Abner" and Kelly's "Pogo" were among the first and most effective critical weapons turned against Joseph R. McCarthy in a time when the popular media seemed frozen in fright by the antics of the junior senator from Wisconsin. With Schulz's "Peanuts," these comic strips did most of the little that was being done by the press to deflate the pompous pretensions of a society that enshrined security and conformity above all else in its decalogue of virtues.

This was a time, too, when a new medium with enormous potential as a social instrument burst upon the American scene. Television opened up whole new dimensions in transmitting both information and commentary to a vaster audience than any other medium had ever commanded. The opportunities it afforded seemed limitless, and some Americans foresaw a whole new era in which this remarkable medium would be used imaginatively and potently to confront the public with a critical analysis of contemporary problems. The novelist, Harvey Swados, in his introduction to an anthology of the writings of the muckrakers, drawing a parallel between the popular magazines for which they wrote and today's television, made this proposal in 1962:

> We ought to try to imagine what it would be like if today's novelists and poets were suddenly to assume leading roles in television, at the invitation of and with the enthusiastic co-operation of the masters of the medium. We ought to try to imagine what it would be like if this collaboration were to exclude the advertisers and their agents from active participation in programming, and were to aim solely at confronting the viewing public evening in and evening out, forcefully and passionately, with words and pictures of the American scene, with tributes to the heroic and assaults on the venal, the cowardly, the exploiting.[4]

Swados's vision has never been realized, of course, nor does it seem likely to be in the foreseeable future. Even more than the publishers of newspapers and magazines, the owners and managers of the television networks have sought not just to please their advertisers, but to avoid offense to even the smallest segment of their potential audience. Social criticism does not lend itself to the achievement of these ends, and not even the easing of tensions which humor and satire have been assumed to provide is acceptable when the subject matter is in the least controversial. The fate of nearly all

[4]Harvey Swados, ed., *Years of Conscience* (Cleveland and New York, 1962), pp. 18–19.

the few television offerings which have attempted to move ever so slightly in this direction (the Smothers Brothers Comedy Hour is, at the moment, the most recent example) would dampen the hopes of the most optimistic believer in the potential of the medium as an outlet for creative and trenchant social criticism in the comic vein.

This is to leave aside the contention of some critics that a more compelling reason for the decline of American humor and satire in modern times is the nature of the times themselves rather than the mass qualities of the media. The blackness and sickness that pervade so much of today's comedy, it is contended, are attributable to the very condition in which man finds himself in this latter half of the twentieth century. His problems are so vast and so pervasive, information concerning them is transmitted to him with such immediacy and so overpoweringly, that no release from the tensions they create is possible except through resort to the bitterest and most ghoulish kind of laughter. His humor, as this school of criticism would have it, has been turned in upon his own deep malaise, and he finds comic only that which is totally depraved.[5] Whether this is humor at all is arguable, and obviously it is not well adapted to the popular media. Thus, today's social critic who would use the weapons of humor and satire is either deprived of a popular vehicle or finds that what he writes is not regarded as meaningful. He has, in either instance, become a critic without an audience.

•   •   •

Where does one look in this bleak and gloomy picture of today's media for hopeful signs that their important function as social critics will not be wholly obliterated? Some may point to the obvious attempt that has been made by federal courts in recent years to create an atmosphere in which the various media might find encouragement to express themselves openly and freely in the role of social critic. In a whole series of decisions, reaching back at least to *New York Times* v. *Sullivan* in 1964, the Supreme Court has clearly been seeking to define in the most liberal manner possible the area within which the press may speak out critically without fear of

---

[5]For a thorough explication of this thesis, see Jesse Bier, *The Rise and Fall of American Humor* (New York, 1968).

punitive civil action. The thrust of these decisions has been to encourage the media to comment candidly on important issues, to give voice to critical and heretical opinion, to stimulate public discussion. In rulings pertaining to libel, the invasion of privacy, obscenity, and other restrictions by which the right of free expression has sometimes been curbed, the courts have repeatedly indicated that they attach a high priority to the importance of permitting a hearing for the most biting criticism, the frankest language. Seldom in our history has the judicial climate seemed so openly favorable to the most literal interpretation of the First Amendment as an instrument for encouraging free expression and stimulating public discussion.

Yet, with few exceptions, there is discouragingly little indication that the media are availing themselves of the new freedom which the courts have, almost literally, thrust upon them. The repressive influence, it seems reasonable to conclude, comes from within the media, rather than from the government, or other external forces. Their mass orientation, which has been a major force in curtailing critical expression, becomes more and more firmly established. Nor, given the combination of the nature of the times and the pervasiveness of the big-audience media, is it possible to look hopefully for any major change in the atmosphere which so clearly limits even our capacity to laugh at our foibles.

Some faint glimmerings of hope have been created in recent years by the growth of a tendency toward specialized audience publications (especially magazines); the occasional success of a journal of personal opinion (Harry Golden's *Carolina Israelite* and Gene Cervi's *Rocky Mountain Journal* are examples); a few weekly newspapers, most of them in metropolitan areas, which have dared depart from the pattern of orthodoxy; and, of course, the underground press, which has certainly not been afraid to take a critical position in relation to just about every aspect of the American society.

It is difficult to measure the impact as social critics of these departures from the media norm. Most share the obvious handicap of a limited audience, though it is well to remember that—even today—the numbers of people reached is not necessarily indicative of the influence the critic may exert. His impact on the thinking of a few thousand individuals could conceivably be a significant force. Yet most of these outlets for social criticism have such miniscule audiences or (as with all but a few of the specialized audience magazines) do not offer a fare much less bland than that of the mass audience publications, that it is hard to be sanguine about their influence.

This would seem to leave the underground press, which has attracted several million readers and has compelled attention far beyond its regular audience, as the last best hope to assume the social critic's role in the United States today. It is totally irreverent, thoroughly iconoclastic. Its audience, mostly young people, is hardly representative of even this sector of the population, but has been an acknowledged force in developments that reach well beyond the college campuses.

It is difficult, however, to take the individual underground publications seriously as effective vehicles for social criticism. With a few notable exceptions, the quality of the product they offer is so shoddy, so badly written, so haphazardly presented as to minimize its appeal, once the initial novelty has worn off. These observations take no account of the obvious and deliberate use by most underground publications of material intended to achieve their ends through shock. Effective social critics of the past have not been averse to using shock as a means of achieving emphasis. But most have recognized that shock—by its very definition—is not accomplished by the endless repetition of those devices now so heavily relied on—obscenity, pornography, scatology, nudity, and all the rest. What is shocking today very soon becomes boring in its hundredth reincarnation—if not its tenth. Ingenuity is a first requisite of shock, and few who write for the underground press today seem to be very ingenious.

What is most discouraging about the little social criticism the media provide today—in all and any of its various limited manifestations—is the dreadful solemnity of most who are engaged in it. This is surely the principal curse of the very few who provide the mass media with the stingy ration of commentary to be found there. So marked is this condition that William F. Buckley, Jr., stands out among them as almost the only one to whom wit and humor are not total strangers, and Buckley, though he does perform the role of social critic, offers little that is meaningful to any but those who share his desire to retreat as rapidly as possible into the repressive safety of the Middle Ages. Russell Baker and Art Buchwald might be cited as exceptions, along with a handful of columnists for newspapers in such diverse places as Des Moines and San Francisco, but they are the tiniest islands in a sea of sepulchral pontification.

Worst of all, it is the younger critics—those who provide the bulk of what appears in the underground press and the few other places where one might hope to find evidence of a new and effective variety of humor and satire—who are most fearsomely solemn in attacking their targets. They are not wanting in fervor and audacity, if only they were not such dreadful bores! Few among them display any appreciation of the efficacy of humor, even if it be used only now and then to achieve contrast. As a result, they wear out their welcomes in a hurry.

If the media today are to assume a measure of responsibility in this vital area of social criticism, what is clearly needed is a rebirth of the talent for humor—particularly in its satiric form—which has characterized those too few periods in the history of the press in the United States when it truly and effectively performed this important function. This is not to pine nostalgically for the appearance of another Petroleum V. Nasby, a Mr. Dooley, or an Archy—none of whom would be acceptable in the role of fool or jester to the audiences of today. The perceptiveness of David Ross Locke, of Finley Peter Dunne, and of Don Marquis was not in the specific characters they created but in their ability to encourage their contemporaries to see through the flaws in their respective societies by making them laugh at what was so patently in need of change.

Today's media reach a larger audience than it has been possible to reach at any previous time. The judicial atmosphere was never so favorable to the free expression of ideas. The times cry out for writers who can expose the paradoxes of an affluent society that can deal with neither poverty nor bigotry. The opportunities for social criticism by the media are boundless, as is the media's neglect to act upon them.

8 PHOTOGRAPHIC COMMUNICATION: AN EVOLVING HISTORICAL DISCIPLINE

R. Smith Schuneman

R. Smith Schuneman, University of Minnesota, is a prolific writer in the areas of photography and graphics and a former head of the Photojournalism Division of the Association for Education in Journalism.

While Americans were enduring the great depression of the 1930s, publishers experimented intensively with a new form of mass communication capable of providing a wealth of description and detail generally not communicable through the written or spoken word. This was photographic communication: photojournalism for newspapers, magazines, and the film, first shown in theaters and later to assume a major role in television.

Man's ability to capture the visual likeness of nature was already a century old when *Life, Look,* and the interpretive newsreel *The March of Time* were introduced in the mid-1930s. But film and still photography had been technological developments which the world-oriented communications industry did not quickly utilize. Editorial methods had been developed to guide use of the *word* in magazines, books, and newspapers. Any illustrations used until the turn of the century had been contributed by hand artists who hardly wished to see their product give way to the photograph. Skilled "word-men"—writers and editors—were firmly entrenched in the "establishment" of the publishing industry; technological change was not readily welcomed in such an environment.

As communicators sought means to interpret and explain the state of the nation in the 1930s, they no doubt became aware of how European publishers were utilizing a sophisticated blend of the written word and still photograph. Significant experimentation with photographic communication then began in America. It blazed a trail which led mass communicators to recognize the value of the visual dimension of a message. Out of this new awareness emerged the picture magazine, the documentary film, and a basic approach to a new medium, television, following World War II.

Just as it can be documented that the institutions of mass communication were slow to recognize the important role of the still and moving image, so also can it be shown that scholars and researchers of communication history have devoted only token attention to the visual mode. For example, the scholarly publication devoted to research in journalism and mass communication, *Journalism Quarterly,* published 1417 articles in the 40-year period 1924–1964. Of these, 37 were devoted to photographic communication! Only 2½ percent of the content of a publication devoted to mass communication was related to the visual dimension of communication research. While the *Quarterly* does not represent a monopoly outlet for communication research, its content indicates the relative inactivity of communication educators and researchers toward the special area of photographic communication.

Certainly, though, any comprehensive review of the literature of photography and film reveals a rather significant collection of books, monographs, and articles on dozens of subtopics. The greatest wealth of material relates to the science of photography and dates to long before Daguerre's announcement of the process in 1839. Authors have also devoted significant thought to the esthetic, the art, of both film and photography. But, on the *history* of film and photography—especially as it can be related to the mass media—there is a paucity of material.

WHAT HAVE HISTORIANS STUDIED ABOUT PHOTOGRAPHIC COMMUNICATION?

Those historians who have concentrated on photographic communication have selected a wide market of topics for research and analysis, but the accumulated research efforts can be given focus by relating them to a familiar paradigm of the communication process. Dr. Harold D. Lasswell, professor of law at Yale and author of *The Communication of Ideas* (1948), suggested that a convenient way to describe an act of communication is to answer:

Who
Says What
In Which Channel
To Whom
With What Effect?

Researchers who concentrate on the *Who*, says Lasswell, are engaged in control analysis. They are studying the communicator—the source of the message—and the factors which initiate or guide his act of communication. *Says What* researchers are performing content analysis, and those who study *In Which Channel* are engaged in media analysis. Study of the *To Whom* segment represents audience analysis. Attempts to determine *With What Effect* are measures of audience impact or effect analysis.

Historical research about communication aspects of photography and film has from the very earliest concentrated on the *Who*. In fact, scholars have been so preoccupied with source research that major collections of original photographs are frequently catalogued only by the name of photographer.

Because still photographers leave such graphic evidence of their thinking, biographies and autobiographies are available on many of the major contributors in the field. Significant autobiographies include Margaret Bourke-White's *Portrait of Myself;* David Douglas Duncan's *Yankee Nomad;* William Henry Jackson's *Time Exposure;* Gordon Parks's *A Choice of Weapons;* and Edward Steichen's *A Life in Photography.*

Biographical studies of historical significance include such works as James Horan's *Mathew Brady: Historian with a Camera* and *Timothy O'Sullivan: America's Forgotten Photographer;* Helmot and Alison Gernsheim's *Roger Fenton;* Judith M. Gutman's *Lewis W. Hine and the American Social Conscience;* Louise Ware's *Jacob A. Riis;* and Richard Griffith's *The World of Robert Flaherty.*

Biographical studies are also being contributed by graduate students of communication history. At the University of Wisconsin, Frederick R. Ellis wrote a 1968 M.A. thesis on "Dickey Chapelle, A Reporter (photographer) and her Work." Fred Bauries, University of Minnesota, contributed "W. Eugene Smith: An Examination of His Career and Philosophy" as a 1967 M.A. thesis.

Such studies frequently examine the photographer's early life and include evidence about the growth of his interest in the medium, his education, and his preparation for the work to follow. Highlights in his career and contributions made by the individual may be described along with an analysis of his specific approach or style. Hypotheses are often formed from having seen a given photographer's work; these hypotheses are confirmed or disproven as the researcher samples in depth.

Biographical research about photographic communicators can provide many interesting experiences and challenges. For example, a member of the staff of the Prints and Photographs Division of the Library of Congress, Milton Kaplan, was recently given a group of 25 important original glass plate negatives taken during the summer of 1863 in South Carolina. He had already co-authored three books, one of which dealt with a photographic history of the Civil War, and had developed an historical method for working with visual forms of communication when he began this intriguing, but puzzling assignment. Who made these plates? When? Why?

> There were photographs of Major General Quincy A. Gillmore (who began the Charleston campaign), a horse and wagon which might have been the photographers' van, and a bombproof, splin-

terproof shelter. In one, the U.S. fleet stands offshore; in another the Confederate flag flies over Fort Sumter.[1]

Examination of the 4¾-by-7½-inch plates which were stored in their original wooden box revealed the names of Haas & Peale scratched into the emulsion on 10 of the 25. Who were they? The names had previously been noted on some copy photos in the Library of Congress collection. Printed captions read "Photo by Haas & Peale, Morris Island and Hilton Head, S. C.," but no one had ever seriously inquired as to who these men were and what their assignments had been.

Milton Kaplan now set out to discover the history behind the men and their work. City directories for Baltimore, Boston, Chicago, Cincinnati, New York, Philadelphia, Pittsburgh, St. Louis, and Washington from the Civil War period were examined for reference to these names without success. A book published in 1865 which dealt with operations in the Charleston area was located, and 14 etchings within were clearly the same as the Haas & Peale plates, but no printed credit line could be found to confirm that Haas & Peale had indeed been the photographers.

Kaplan next wrote the publisher of that 1865 book only to receive a reply that all records pertaining to the book had been destroyed by fire in 1893. Next an exhaustive study was made of the regimental histories of units serving in the Charleston campaign. Some of the Haas & Peale photographs again appeared as etched reproductions, but no references or credit lines were given.

A study of other Civil War books turned up reproductions of several Haas & Peale photographs in each of four books. Only in one was there a credit line for a photograph which matched one of the glass plates. It read "This picture is from a photograph by Samuel A. Cooley, photographer of the Fourth Army Corps." Researcher Kaplan then entertained the very serious question of whether Haas & Peale had made any of the glass plates. Was the credit line in error?

A search in the National Archives turned out both stereographs

[1]Milton Kaplan, "The Case of the Disappearing Photographers," *The Quarterly Journal of the Library of Congress* 24 (January 1967), 40–45. References to this particular study rely upon a personal interview with the author as well as the published article.

and photographs taken by Cooley on Morris Island in 1864. Cooley had photographed some of the same landmarks as revealed in the Haas & Peale glass plates; however, shell damage was clearly greater in the 1864 Cooley stereographs and photographs than in the Haas & Peale plates. Thus, it was likely—but not certain—that the credit line for Cooley was in error. Cooley had probably not photographed these landmarks until 1864, after Haas and Peale made their plates.

Next the researcher scanned each issue of the *New York Herald* and *Frank Leslie's Illustrated Newspaper* for any information or references to photographic work in the Morris Island area from July to November 1863. There was no information. A similar search in *Harper's Weekly* provided the first solid lead in this complicated bit of research. The August 15, 1863, issue referred to a woodcut of General Gillmore as "based upon a photograph credited to a *Lieutenant* Haas."

A search back at the National Archives identified the lieutenant as Philip Haas, Company A, 1st New York Engineers, enlisted, September 1861. Also in the Archives was found an order book of the 1st New York Engineers which contained:

> A Special Order No. 248, dated July 15, 1862, Hilton Head, Port Royal, detailing Haas for "special service at headquarters." On file also is a letter from Haas, dated May 13, 1862, Tybee Island, in which he asks for "a leave of absence for thirty days to go north—my supply of photographic material being entirely exhausted (sic) which require to be selected with great care." Another letter dated November 5, 1862, requesting leave on account of ill health is signed "Philip Haas . . . Photographer, General Staff." A comparison of the signatures on the two letters with the name on the negatives reveals certain similarities.[2]

Kaplan also found other letters: One requested a carpenter for work in the "Photographic Bureau" and another requested an assistant. When Haas resigned from the Army May 25, 1863, he left a letter requesting the Quartermaster to take charge of photographic equipment he had been using, "they being government property."

Milton Kaplan, photographic researcher, had found enough evidence to conclude that the Haas of Haas & Peale was, indeed, Lt. Philip Haas. The George Eastman House in Rochester, New York, has in its possession—as do the Library of Congress and National Archives—photographs mounted on special printed cards with the imprint "Photo by Haas & Peale, Morris Island and Hilton Head, S. C."

A part of the mystery has been solved, but more, indeed must be learned before the story nears completion. Who was Peale? And where was the firm Haas and Peale? Here, then, remains a ready-made piece of source research for anyone interested in adding to our knowledge of the photographic documentation of the War Between the States.

Another interesting study requiring source research involves the work of a French photographer, Eugene Atget (1856–1927). Atget documented life and architectural details along the streets of Paris, though his work did not receive serious attention until after his death. At that time a New York photographer, Berenice Abbott, who had known Atget while herself working in Paris, purchased Atget's glass plate negatives which were stored in an attic. She brought the collection of several thousand prints and approximately 1000 glass plates to this country and published a portfolio of Atget's work.

Then, in 1968, the Museum of Modern Art Department of Photography purchased the entire collection from Miss Abbott and Julian Levy. An archivist in charge of the Museum's new collection, Yolanda Hershey, first catalogued the work and then, in late 1969, traveled to Paris to seek additional biographical information about Atget from those who remembered him. Mrs. Hershey also photographed many of the streets and buildings once captured by Atget. Her problem was to identify the locations of as many of Atget's views as possible, though a half century or more separated her documentation from the time of Atget's activity.

This study has additional interest to the historical researcher because it represents analysis of two parts of the Lasswell paradigm: control analysis (source research) as well as content analysis. While Mrs. Hershey interviewed those who remembered Atget and his methods of work, she was adding to knowledge about the communicator. But, as she studied the original Atget photographs and then searched for the similar images in 1969, she was involved in a study of the message.

Most of the biographies and autobiographies contain such a blend of control and content analysis. How can one understand the life, contributions, and approach of a communicator without also study-ing his product, communication?

A careful search for historical studies which have a decided content-analytic approach yielded wide variations in the kinds of in-formation sought when messages, though visual, are examined. One researcher might study photographs for certain stylistic elements (viewpoint, lighting, attention to edge and frame, visual organiza-tion, control of motion, treatment of background-foreground relation-ships, etc.); the analysis of graphic design and layout is another frequent topic. Images may, on the other hand, be analyzed in terms of subject. A researcher might be looking for the relative at-tention paid to Negroes vs. Caucasians, men-women-children, or com-mon people vs. celebrities. Perhaps the analyst is looking for evi-dence of violence, graffiti, historical landmarks, the clothing of the day. The researcher interested in film or television may analyze the editor's control and manipulation of time: e.g. juxtaposition of scenes, visual continuity, cutting, etc. Or, he may examine propa-ganda films to determine techniques of persuasion employed by the producers. He may be looking for stylistic elements of production or qualities of subject as with the still photograph. His analysis may be extended to consideration of the sound track.

One researcher, Jane Trahey, recently undertook a content-analytic study of the bound volumes of *Harper's Bazaar* in search of visual and written material for her book *Harper's Bazaar: 100 Years of the American Female*. In her introduction, she revealed the many differ-ent content-analytic avenues (though she did not quite use those terms!) one might take with a century of material. A book could be drawn from *Bazaar*'s leadership in graphic design. How many maga-zines could boast such important names as Erté, Brodovitch, Henry Wolf, Marvin Israel, Ruth Ansel, and Bea Feitler? One could easily focus another book on photographic contributions to the maga-zine by such greats as Eugene Atget, Baron de Meyer, Munkacsi, Cartier-Bresson, Man Ray, Hoyingen-Huene, Louise Dahl-Wolfe, Saul Leiter, Hiro, Sieff, and the undisputed leader of fashion pho-tography, Richard Avedon. Why not also do a book on just the cartoons? Or the fashions? Or the models? Any of these would not only be interesting, but would most certainly provide a visual in-sight into both the contents of the magazine and those who con-tributed to it.

Milton Kaplan, the Library of Congress researcher who sought an answer to the Haas & Peale mystery, collaborated with Stephen Hess in researching a history of American political cartoons. Titled *The Ungentlemanly Art* (1968), the work begins with the first-known American political cartoon (drawn by none other than Benjamin Franklin in 1747), continues to Paul Revere's cartoon of the Boston Massacre, Thomas Nast's fight against the Tweed Ring, and the work of such contemporary masters as Herblock and Mauldin. The authors searched broadsides, magazines, and newspapers, and they reveal how the cartoon has evolved as persuasive visual communication. The research technique was historic and content analytic.

Another visual content analysis of historic importance was completed by Van Deren Coke, a professor of art at the University of New Mexico. Professor Coke recently contributed a book, *The Painter and the Photograph* (1964), in which he confirmed his hypothesis that the photograph represents for the painter a new way of seeing. It provides the painter with a quite different visual library of images than those stored in his mind from direct experience. Coke presented pairs of images—a photograph and a painting—to document the graphic influence exerted by photographs upon selected painters' finished works, not only in detail, but in style and approach as well. Of course, all photographs used as evidence were made prior in time to a painter's work on the same subject.

Such conclusive evidence as Coke presented required a thorough substantive knowledge of the histories of painting and photography. It also required the research methodology of a content analyst, in this case a *visual* analyst, an historical researcher with sophistication in design, representation, and photography.

An important study which is both historical and theoretical in its conclusions is *The Photographer's Eye* by John Szarkowski (1966). Szarkowski, now director of the Department of Photography at the Museum of Modern Art in New York City, drew upon photographs made over a period of 125 years by the known and unknown, the artist and snapshooter, the photographic poet and the documentarian. What Szarkowski sought was, in a sense, a content-analytic scheme for classifying uniquely photographic qualities of camera-made images. He wanted to determine those visual criteria which seemed inherent in the photographic medium. Once these criteria could be isolated and identified, Szarkowski reasoned, then would there not exist a kind of theoretical structure within which the history and development of the medium could be judged? The five visual criteria researched and presented in *The Photographer's Eye* are: (a) The Thing Itself, (b) The Detail, (c) The Frame, (d) Time, and (e) Vantage Point.

Szarkowski defined each criterion at the beginning of its unit in the book. Then he presented his evidence in photographic form, requiring the viewer to examine carefully each image to determine if it exhibited the referent criterion. If the viewer thought such a criterion was present, it next became his responsibility to identify specific visual clues and determine their validity. Szarkowski's selections leave most readers certain of the validity of the five qualities defined; readers probably also conclude that other visual qualities or criteria exist. As the content-analytic "code book" can be expanded and refined along the lines suggested by Szarkowski, visual historians may look to this approach as a method of analyzing dimensions of the development of photographic communication. What is most significant about Szarkowski's work is that implicitly it sets out to establish "historical standards" for judging development of photographic communication.[3]

An interesting variation of the content-analytic technique of historical research involves a study of what was *not* shown to an audience of a mass medium—"the film on the cutting-room floor," so to speak. This writer recently spent more than a month in photographic repositories in the eastern United States searching specifically for images which newspaper or magazine audiences had never seen.

For example nearly everyone is familiar with the very moving and emotional photograph of the "migrant mother" and children made by Dorothea Lange in the depression years. The photograph is one of the most widely published from that period. But what other images did Miss Lange record that late afternoon in March 1936, near Nipomo, California? How did she find this mother of seven children? Were any of the photographs "set-up" or posed?

---

[3]See L. John Martin and Harold L. Nelson, "The Historical Standard in Analyzing Press Performance," *Journalism Quarterly* 33 (1956) 456–466, for an explanation of the historical standard and its use by communication researchers.

Five photographs could be found from Lange's "take" involving the migrant mother and her children. An examination of them—four unpublished—revealed many more visual details about the family than the well-known image: their tent; the children playing near it; a mother nursing her baby just inside the open front; a close-up of the mother with baby-in arms and one child at her shoulder who was looking toward the camera; and finally the classic photograph of the mother, baby-in-arms, and two children at her shoulders, both turned away.[4] Included with the caption material was the following:

> Migrant agricultural worker's family. Seven hungry children. Mother aged 32, the father is a native Californian. Destitute in a pea-pickers camp because of the failure of the early pea crop. These people had just sold their tent in order to buy food. Most of the 2500 people in this camp were destitute.

In this instance, there is a far more comprehensive understanding of this family's situation after seeing the four unpublished photos and learning from the caption material that the family's sole form of shelter soon was to be taken. The classic published photograph gains in emotional impact, for the reader has been provided context.

This is quite a different approach to content analysis. It represents studying not only content submitted to an audience, but also that which the audience did not have an opportunity to see. Such studies are often referred to as "gatekeeper" studies by communication researchers, for they represent an examination of the content held back by the editor—the "gatekeeper."

Content analysis is used by historians in the evaluation of the film and television as well. While A. William Bluem's *Documentary in American Television* (1965) is a synthesis, it indeed utilizes content-analytic findings frequently in its evaluations of documentary films.

Bluem analyzed the Robert Drew Associates production of "The

---

[4]There is firm evidence that other negatives were made, but they have never been printed—nor can they be. Each negative was judged by someone of the Historical Branch staff as to whether or not it was of use for the F.S.A. file at that time. Those negatives which were judged of value were printed, and it is those prints which are housed in the Library of Congress. A duplicate set was placed in the New York Public Library, though the collection there is not so complete. Those negatives judged not of value were physically "punched" and rendered unprintable, a fact of itself worthy of a lengthy and intensive investigation and report for an historical journal.

Chair" (the case of Paul Crump, a Negro convicted of murder, first sentenced to die, and later given life-in-prison) as follows:

> The difference between "The Chair" and a typical *Perry Mason* segment is dramaturgically small—and yet the severe distinction between them is that nothing seen in the "The Chair" was not made from the raw material of life. In that difference lies still another testimony to *verité*. On two occasions, for example, the attorney totally forgot the camera and sound equipment. At one point he learned, in a telephone conversation, that a highly placed community leader planned to make a public statement in behalf of Crump's commutation—a stroke of good fortune beyond his wildest hopes. The conversation ended and suddenly he was in tears, a reaction so intense and natural that it was a full minute before he recalled the camera's presence. Not since the early *Philco Playhouse* production of . . . *The Haven* did one see a more naturally motivated analysis of a man so deeply moved that he wept before us—and only with great concentration can we remember that one was a drama and the other the revelation of a real man intensely involved in a real situation.[5]

One recent master's thesis involving a study of communication through film was "A Qualitative Content Analysis of the Relationship of Visual and Sound in Four Documentary Films Produced During the Past 30 Years" by Sister Patricia A. Cyra, Marquette University, 1968. Here the method of historical investigation clearly relies on content analysis to give us additional insight into multichannel messages and their development.

This writer himself developed much of an historical doctoral thesis at the University of Minnesota around content-analytic methodology, both quantitative and qualitative. Titled *The Photograph in Print: An Examination of New York Daily Newspapers 1890–1937* (1967), the thesis defines trends in newspaper news and editorial photojournalism. Identification of major changes in the content, subject, size, and volume of use of pictures involved utilization of quantitative techniques. The study of the development of technical innovations and visual characteristics of photographs and picture layouts in print relied on qualitative content analysis.

[5]A. William Bluem, *Documentary in American Television* (New York, 1965), p. 198.

For the quantitative phase of the study about 11,500 photographs were analyzed from more than 8,600 newspaper pages. Dates for analysis were drawn according to techniques of sampling and statistics well tested and proven by scholars. Thirteen newspaper titles were involved. A number of "pilot studies" were completed in advance of the main study to test each of the content categories and allow for their articulation.

The qualitative data were gathered from the same titles, but this time a sample of 50 landmark or "major event" dates from 1890 through 1937 was relied upon. How the newspapers performed in their use of the photograph in covering each of the 50 events was qualitatively assessed. This phase of the study relied heavily upon the investigator's acquired knowledge of the history of the technologies of photography, photoengraving, and printing, as well as the histories of art, photography, and journalism.

Historians of photographic communication have thus been shown to involve themselves in examination of the first two ingredients of the Lasswell paradigm: the *Who* and *Says What* components. They are also concerned with *In Which Channel* research as will be evident in the following examination of historical studies of the media themselves.

While not any great number of studies about photographic communication involve media analysis, some of the very finest scholarship has been so directed. And, just as one often finds combination studies involving examination of both the communicator and his message (control and content analysis), so also is the combined analysis of the message and medium both desirable and convenient (content and media analysis). The reason for this mix is similar in its logic to that given for combining control and content analysis: How can one study a medium of transmission without also examining what it is called upon to transmit? Or, to put it in the terms of Marshall McLuhan, "The Medium is the Message."

One of the very best historic and theoretical analyses of the photojournalistic medium was contributed by Wilson Hicks in *Words and Pictures* (1952). Hicks set forth, in an historical context, the first definitive theory of the process of word-and-photograph communication (multichannel). He addressed himself to a comparison of the roles of the word and the image in print-media communication. His analysis led to a definition of the nature of the content which could best be transmitted over each of the two channels involved in ink-on-paper journalism. He supported his theory with historical evidence, tracing the development of the use of words and pictures from European publications to magazines in the United States. The work remains a classic, particularly the first unit.

Another work centered on media analysis is Nathan Lyon's anthology *Photographers on Photography* (1966), which presents 40 previously published periodical contributions covering about a century of the history of the photographic medium. Of particular value to the historian of photographic communication are Wynn Bullock, "Space and Time"; Henri Cartier-Bresson, "Introduction to the Decisive Moment"; Henry Holmes Smith, "Photography in our Time"; and W. Eugene Smith, "Photographic Journalism." While these studies are very personal, hypothetical, and somewhat philosophic, they do represent thoughtful analyses on the nature of the medium by creative producers of photography.

Two doctoral theses which represent the highest quality of scholarship in the history of photographic communication and deal with media analysis are Otha Spencer, *Twenty Years of Life: A Study of Time, Inc.'s Picture Magazine and Its Contributions to Photojournalism* (1958) and Robert Kahan, *The Antecedents of American Photojournalism* (1969). Spencer received his doctor's degree from the University of Missouri; Kahan from the University of Wisconsin.

The search for primary documents took Spencer directly to Time-Life in New York City, where he gained access to both the men and the evidence necessary to define the events surrounding the founding of *Life* in 1936 and to help him in assessing it as a medium of photojournalism during its first 20 years. Time-Life archives were opened to Spencer, who retrieved the essence of thought and policy which led to Henry Luce's final decision to found the weekly picture magazine. There were interviews and correspondence of those who had a direct hand in *Life*'s start: such pioneers as Alex Groner, Time-Life historian; Kurt Safranski, an important European picture-magazine editor from the House of Ullstein; and Daniel Longwell, *Life*'s first editor.

In the thesis, the reader can develop a comprehensive understanding of the group-journalism process and the nature of a picture magazine produced in such an environment. Spencer's work represents a depth and intensity of historical research worthy of careful study by those seeking to develop similar research skills.

The thesis of Robert Kahan also represents a skilled retrieval of documentary evidence to profile the nature of photojournalism in the mass-circulation magazine during the 1880s and 1890s. Kahan shows particular savvy in his command of late nineteenth century periodical literature (much of it unindexed).

A master's thesis which is centered on media analysis, but concerned with the film rather than still photograph, is Martin A. Rennalls's "Development of the Documentary Film in Jamaica," Boston University, 1968.

A comprehensive and worldwide analysis of film has been contributed by Paul Rotha and Richard Griffith in *The Film Till Now* (1967). This critical survey, which covers the "literature of film" over a 60-year period, was first published in 1930 and has been expanded in each of three subsequent editions. A majority of the book deals with historic development of the film as a communication medium; other chapters are devoted to lists of production units, a glossary of terms, and descriptions of production techniques. One could not defend the work as solely media and/or content analysis; it is a synthesis. Some attention is paid to communicators at the one end of the paradigm and at the other end of the continuum it occasionally reaches into audiences and effects. Its dominant contribution, however, is to the historical analysis of the film as a communication medium, thus qualifying for inclusion here.

As one reviews the literature of the history of photographic communication, it is revealing—though certainly disappointing—to discover two divisions of the Lasswell paradigm all but devoid of research attention. Reference is, of course, to the remaining categories: *To Whom* and *With What Effect* (audience and effect analysis).

With reference to the still photograph, audience analyses have been completed periodically for publishers of both newspapers and magazines. Cited by Spencer in his examination of *Life* are audience analyses by an independent commercial research agency on such topics as "The Accumulative Audience of *Life*," "The Household Accumulative Audience of *Life*," "A Study of Four Media," and "A Study of Duplication." Similar studies are done by most major publishers at regular intervals, and results are generally available for research purposes. An historian working with such audience analyses would most probably approach the data as a longitudinal or developmental study. He would frequently be disappointed, though, for each commercial study is devoted to data which concentrate on one or two themes. Those particular themes may not ever be repeated in subsequent field work.

Media owners, as well as the institutions of advertising, have been willing to expend sizable budgets for audience and effects research, but these have, for the most part, been cross-sectional rather than longitudinal and have been oriented to specific problems. Historians interested in audience or effect analysis have not found it economically feasible to conduct field surveys of their own over the time period necessary to provide data for trend examination.

From this review, it becomes quite clear that the major research effort of photographic historians has been biographic, dealing with the communicator himself. Attention has also been directed rather recently to content and media analyses, though from the universe of possible and important studies the surface has hardly been scratched. For both economic and methodological reasons, little if any attention has been directed by communication historians to audience and effects studies. Certainly the time has come in this day of emphasis upon interdisciplinary research approaches for the quantifier and the qualifier—the behavioralist and historian—to join in data-gathering and interpretation related to the audiences and effects of photographic communication.

WHAT NEW PROBLEMS SHOULD BE STUDIED?

Too much of our research literature has been descriptive rather than analytic. It has been the handsomely printed exhibit catalog or collection of photographs without comment, criticism, or analytic scheme. Someone retrieved; period. Perhaps it has been a composite reel of one producer's films. As for analysis, there is none. Why have interpretation and analysis been so greatly slighted?

Of course, it is important that researchers provide descriptive studies of events and contributions of the past. But it is urgent that through interpretation and analysis they also communicate the significance of descriptive findings. A well-known senior professor of mass communications recently asked this writer if it were as valuable for graduate students of photographic communication "to learn about old photographers and their pictures as compared to learning about contemporary communication theory." His concept of the level of sophistication of the history of photographic communication—and hence, by inference, the value of content available to students in the classroom—was clearly indicative of the problem. A quick and internalized reply was that the study of history does not mean just "old photographers and their pictures." It means the opportunity to relate and evaluate the *significance* of the wealth of contributions to the problems facing the creative communicator, his medium, and his message today. That, it seems, is the challenge to historical researchers; to make their findings and interpretations revelant (sic)! Why should anyone learn about a Horace Greeley or a Ben Franklin, much less research and analyze the man and his work? Is it justifiable or defensible to say it is important *today* because someone or his work *was important yesterday*? Hardly, in this day of information explosion. The historian must retrieve facts, yes; but he must *reveal principles* through analysis and presentation in a context which his audience can identify as *relevant today*.

Turning to the specific topics and problem areas, to which historical researchers of photographic communication ought to be addressing themselves, is difficult only because the needs are so broad.

Film is the new, dynamic medium of communication which is of intense interest to young, creative minds. Many high school, undergraduate, and graduate students have a thirst to learn of the heritage of film—its development as a medium of persuasion, information, and entertainment. But precious little is available to those who seek. It is a medium to which photographic historians should devote serious attention.

A particular criticism of most historical studies of *film* is that they have used *printed* media as transmission channels, a factor which imposes unnatural restrictions and artificial boundaries on the essence of what may be communicated.

Film is a visual mode with three dimensions: length, width, and time. Transmission of findings must utilize a comparable mode and dimension. Many studies must thus be presented on video tape or film if audiences are to reap full benefit from the researchers' findings.

How can a student of film history appreciate the work of such pioneers in film making as Robert Flaherty if he has access only to a words-on-paper analysis giving such important, but nonvisual details as the location where Flaherty filmed, descriptions of the things he shot, and his basic approach to editing. Of much greater value to the consumer of film history would be filmic examples selected by the researcher, showing Flaherty's shooting or editing, his intakes and outs. Those examples should be accompanied by appropriate narration, emphasizing the significance of findings presented. Research about the communicator, the content, and the medium of film itself may all be transmitted with greater effectiveness and fidelity on film or video tape than on the printed page.

There is also a need for expanded effort in the analysis of photographic communication in the printed media. There is no definitive study of *Look* magazine comparable to the Otha Spencer thesis on *Life's* first 20 years. Nor are there analyses of the many American picture magazines which preceded *Life*: *Mid-Week Pictorial* and *Current History* (*New York Times*, 1914), *Every Week* (1914), *Panorama* (1929), *Roto* (1934), and many others. After *Life's* founding in 1936, picture magazines which followed and about which little is known included *Click, Photo History, Pic, Peek,* and *Focus.*

At the beginning of the 1970s, there appears to be a kind of "crisis" in photojournalism which photographic historians should be acknowledging in their selection of topics for analysis. In the decades of the 1950s and 1960s such major magazines as *Collier's* and *Saturday Evening Post* vanished. Both were important transmitters of the photojounalistic form. Where will the reader go who desires the quality photographic essay or crusading documentary picture story? Are there historical indices waiting for identification and analysis which might shed light on whether the content traditionally carried by a picture magazine will be assumed by newspapers or other magazine classes or broadcast facsimile? Historians could help both media and consumers by providing an historical base for the decisions and modifications to come. Such studies might be either media or content analytic in nature.

Perhaps neither approach would get to what some hypothesize is at the real root of the problem: economics. An analysis of selected economic variables of import to general-interest magazines would give useful trends.

There is also a "market" for information on how the visual media *interact.* Could a developmental study help in identifying inherent qualities of each of the media with regard to such factors as content, function, etc.?

The communication "gatekeeper" is most worthy of historical examination, particularly in photographic communication. Photographers consistently complain (and frequently believe) that editors weaken rather than strengthen their contributions. A gatekeeper decision is made each time someone determines what will (or will not) reach the audience. He may be the photographer, editor, art director, publisher, or network vice-president. How has he behaved?

Is it true, for example, that *most* prize-winning newspaper photographs have initially been rejected for publication by editors at the time they were made? Photographers claim so. George Thames, who has covered the White House for the *New York Times* since 1946, by 1960 had won some 37 awards in various national competitions. Of those only *seven* had appeared in the *Times* before winning contests!

Again, during the 1968 Democratic National Convention in Chicago, there was criticism of "one-sided" television reporting of violence as seen in newsfilm and videotape coverage. Some television journalists have claimed that "technical problems" limited what they could film and televize of the provocation of police by citizens. However, tape and film editors have admitted that images of provocation were recorded, but, because of audio and visual obscenities, film and tape were edited and the provocation was never aired. Pictures of police clubbing citizens did appear on home sets. Viewers were implicitly asked to believe that the police simply moved in with clubs swinging. The television reports were out of balance—a penalty paid in return for editing out obscenities, judged by the gatekeepers as too offensive to members of the audience to warrant airing. Other gatekeepers have defended that editing as required by law, for FCC regulations forbid airing obscenities. In this case isn't that FCC rule in conflict with the First Amendment? Regardless, this incident clearly did represent the kind of control of content which the gatekeepers of communication may exert. It is a kind of control well deserving historical analysis.

Any search of the published literature reveals that no one has produced a monograph or journal article on the development of agencies, syndicates, and wire services for photographic communication. There is a rich history which should be researched and published.

By the turn of the century such picture services as Bain's (founded c. 1895), Brown Brothers (founded c. 1904), and Underwood & Underwood were supplying photographs to newspapers and magazines. Two of those three were continuing as "stock" picture suppliers at the beginning of the 1970s. Other important syndicates which specifically served newspapers included Wide World, Acme, Pacific, and Atlantic. New York assignment agencies such as Black Star, Magnum, and Pix which have served the photographic needs of magazines ought be included in any study of the development of picture syndicates and agencies.

Equally important and fascinating are the beginnings of wire transmission of photographs in Europe as early as 1907, radio transmission of images across the Atlantic in 1921, and point-to-point wire transmission of photos in the United States in 1924. All preceded Wirephoto in 1935. Hearst's International News Photos, United Press, and the AP developed wire and radio services.

What have these institutions contributed? What wealth of visual material is available from them for those in need of pictures of historical significance? Did the coming of the wire picture services force agencies, such as Brown Brothers and Underwood, to abandon their photographic documentation of current events, thus becoming "stock" picture houses? Have archives for the film been established? What and where are they? These are but a few of the questions historians should be answering about these supporting agencies of photographic communication.

Little material is available to American students on the history of photographic communication for other countries of the world. Studies of central European developments are highest on the priority list of needs, followed closely by studies of Russian, Japanese, South American, and African histories. Clearly, at a time when communication satellites make possible the instantaneous international exchange of moving images, we ought understand the nature of photographic communication and its state of development in other cultures.

In summary, it can be said that there are vast frontiers of photographic communication awaiting historical analysis by students of the mass media. Interest in the visual mode is expanding at a feverish pace. Researchers are thus challenged to energetically provide necessary intellectual stimulation to support that spirit. Analysis of the history of the film and photography, though, presents some serious and quite unique source-availability and methodological problems which now deserve careful attention.

AN EXAMINATION OF METHODS FOR RESEARCH

The researcher who works with written documents—diaries, newspapers, and letters, to name a few—is easily able to carry from a repository a duplicate or near-duplicate record of relevant findings. The record may be in the traditional form of handwritten notes or in contemporary form: Xerox print-outs, microfilm copies, and verbal dictation onto audio tape. Whatever form he chooses, the scholar who works with written documents faces no serious obstacles in abstracting from word sources.

However, a researcher dealing with photographic communication faces quite a different group of problems. Suppose he is interested in a specific work by the film-maker Robert Flaherty. His first problem is to locate a repository which holds the film. Chances are most likely that the film will not be available for circulation, or even "interlibrary" loans. Thus, he will be required to physically travel to the repository if he is to examine that particular film.

He may project the footage at the archives, let us assume, as many times as he chooses. Of course, there are no restrictions on what *written* notes he makes, but he wishes to retrieve and then communicate the visual essence of Flaherty's work. The written word can be a supporting tool, but not the primary one. Somehow he needs to retrieve selections from the film. While it is possible at a very few archives to purchase duplicate films, not copyrighted or otherwise restricted, this is the exception. Resource centers with film collections ought to be equipped with videotape recorders and film chains for electronic transcription of uncopyrighted works. The transcriptions could be loaned to the researcher for a fee covering depreciation on the tape as well as transcription and handling costs. The borrower would return the recording to the repository after use. Materials not covered by copyright also should be available on videotape for purchase from those repositories. Until the U.S. Congress modifies and clarifies the present Copyright Law, little progress can be made in improving availability of copyrighted film.

The earliest television, of course, could only be filmed on 16 mm kinescopes, and many of those programs have been preserved. They may be screened on a standard 16 mm sound motion picture projector. After the introduction of videotape in 1956—an electronic recording process which nearly matches live programming in technical quality—the use of kinescopes all but died, as did preservation of much of video history.

Study of videotape recordings from film, tape, or studio sources today presents the most complicated problem of retrieval for the historian of photographic communication. The high cost of each one-hour roll of videotape (approximately $175) and the complex equipment required have prevented either commercial broadcasters or public and private institutions from preserving more of television programs. One exception is a Minneapolis-St. Paul, Minnesota, commercial station which contributes a limited number of videotape recordings, of what its station officials deemed "historically significant" by station officials, to the Minnesota Historical Society. It is an important and generous service which hopefully will be emulated by other commercial broadcasters.

The photograph is in many ways similar to the film, for its message cannot easily be translated into word-notes. Many photographs published in the mass media are readily available in bound volumes at libraries across the nation, but of course, the image is a photo-mechanically engraved reproduction, a "generation" away from its original form. And, photographs which did not appear in print can only be studied as originals. It should be conceded, though, that study of the still photograph does not present as many serious problems as film or videotape.

Some repositories will allow researchers to make their own photographic copies of prints in their collection. Copyrighted materials cannot, of course, be published under any circumstances without written permission from an owner. Those photographs in the public domain may be copied and published without further concern. A gray area exists for those uncopyrighted prints which have been sold to a repository by a photographer who still retains ownership of the original negative. Can the repository *ethically* allow a researcher to copy a print in the collection, publish it, and hence circumvent compensating the photographer? Most museums, libraries, and archives maintain in such cases that photographs in their collections may be copied, but it is then the responsibility of the researcher to seek permission from the owner of the negative before publication. When the photographer dies, all but very important individual works or portfolios seem to move into public domain, thus not requiring publication permission.

The Library of Congress will make available prints from any negative in its collection at nominal cost. All such images are in the public domain and may be published without further permission. One collector of photography—the Museum of Modern Art of New York City—will allow no scholar or researcher to copy any of the photographs in the collection of their Department of Photography. While scholars are welcome to examine original works in the Steichen Study Center, the no-copy limitation seriously reduces the usefulness of that important source of photographic history. Their restriction is enforced, they report, to protect beyond question a photographer's rights to compensation for images he has made. An interesting contrast to the position of the Museum's Photography Department is the Museum's Department of Film, which *circulates* a rich collection of American and European films.

In summarizing methodological problems facing the historian of photographic communication it seems clear that one of the most important research tools he can possess is a command of the processes and techniques of photography, film, and electography (videotape). Whether he will make high-fidelity copies of original photographs in an archives or supervise a tape-transcription of a 16 mm film, the knowledge of the photographic and electronic recording processes will aid him in retrieving, preserving, and presenting his visual research efforts.

AN EXAMINATION OF VISUAL SOURCES

It is imperative for the serious scholar of historical communication to work from original sources, yet the field is so specialized that only a very limited number of archives and repositories exist. This capsulized "field trip" of sources in the United States is given as a final "thrust" in the hope that it will start graduate students on the trail of the history of photography or film.

There is one institution in the United States devoted to the history of all of photographic communication: its science, art, and functional use; for scholar, hobbyist, or the "just curious." It is the George Eastman House of Photography in Rochester, New York.

This unique photographic museum opened its doors in 1949 with a basic collection of apparatus, prints, and books. Since that time subsequent contributions and acquisitions have brought it to national attention as a most important research center. There are three permanent exhibitions on the "Science and Technology of Photography," "Popular Photography," and "The Art of Photography." The museum is under the direction of Beaumont Newhall, author of the definitive *History of Photography from 1839 to the Present Day* (1964).

On the top floor is the Research Center, which houses a library of more than 8000 volumes and periodicals on photography. The Center is open on special application and by appointment to qualified researchers. Also in the Center is the permanent photographic print collection, which may be studied by those utilizing the facility. Special arrangements may be made for researchers working there to acquire photographic copies of prints of special interest.

The best collection of the work of Lewis W. Hine is at Eastman House. Also well represented are Walker Evans, Eugene Atget, Bruce Davidson, and Felix Man, to name but a few of those photographers of specific interest to photojournalists.

Motion-picture archives are at Eastman House as well. Active collaboration with film archives throughout the world is maintained, and over one million still photos and an additional book library further document the history of film. Films are not circulated, but the Dryden Film Society exhibits in a 500-seat theater which was added in 1950.

The Library of Congress Prints and Photographs Division in Washington, D. C., includes a vast collection of 2.5 million items of nonbook pictorial materials, excluding maps and motion pictures. The booklet *Guide to the Special Collections of Prints and Photographs in the Library of Congress,* compiled by Paul Vanderbilt in 1955, is available from the Superintendent of Documents, U.S. Government Printing Office, Washington, D. C. for $1.25.

Of special interest to the photographic historian is the collection of Civil War photographs, which includes the work of Mathew Brady, Timothy O'Sullivan, Alexander Gardner, George Barnard, and Captain A. J. Russell. A catalog of copy negatives made from originals selected from the Mathew B. Brady collection is available to give the researcher a guide into those holdings. *Civil War Photographs, 1861–1865* is available for 75 cents from the Photoduplication Service, Library of Congress. A 35 mm positive microfilm containing all the photographs described in the catalog is also available from the Photoduplication Service at $20 per copy. This microfilm allows the researcher to examine the visual nature of each picture, an invaluable aid in selection. If all repositories had such films available, new ground could be broken far more rapidly and at a fraction of the present expense.

A collection at the Library of Congress of original Roger Fenton albumen prints from the Crimean War is also important to mid-nineteenth-century historians.

The Library of Congress no doubt holds the most comprehensive collection of work by Arnold Genthe in existence. Of particular interest is Genthe's documentation of the San Francisco earthquake in 1906 and his portraits of Chinatown.

Also, the Farm Security Administration photographs from the 1930s are housed here, as are Office of War Information photographs from World War II. Approximately 272,000 negatives were made by photographers working in the Farm Security Administration Historical Branch during the period. Of these negatives, approximately 150,000 were printed.

A comprehensive examination of work from the depression years by Dorothea Lange, Russell Lee, Arthur Rothstein, Walker Evans, Gordon Parks, Carl Mydans, and John Vachon—to name but a few —awaits photographic historians. Retrieval of photographs by individual photographer is cumbersome and difficult, to say the least, but for the researcher with time and patience, a majority of the images of any one photographer can be located. The Library of Congress also maintains a broad film acquisitions program, preserves motion pictures and related descriptive material, and provides a study center for the use of researchers.

The motion-picture collection of the Library is large and unique in many respects. The greater part of the collection is American; films acquired from Germany, Italy, and Japan during World War II are also available for study. About 32,000 separate films are in the custody of the Motion Picture Section of the Prints and Photographs Division. The collection is maintained primarily for scholarly study and research; public projection and loan service are not available. Serious users are well advised to correspond with the Library concerning specific needs and to request that a schedule of appointments be set up for use of the reference facilities. Copies of films not covered by copyright or otherwise restricted may be purchased. The Allen collection of documentary films and samples of NET productions are only two of many specialized groupings in the Motion Picture Section which may be of interest to historians of photographic communication.

The copyright Cataloging Division in the Copyright Office prepares a semiannual *Catalog of Copyright Entries: Motion Pictures and Filmstrips,* which lists all such materials registered for copyright in the United States. It is published by the Library and sold by the Government Printing Office. The Copyright Office has also prepared four cumulative catalogs entitled *Motion Pictures,* which together cover registrations of films for the years 1894–1959. This work is also available from the Government Printing Office.[6]

Other film archives which should be noted include the British Film Institute, London; the Cinematheque Française, Paris; Reichsfilmarchive, Berlin; Museum of Modern Art Film Library New York; and, finally, the Canadian Film Institute Archives committee. These national archives are all members of the International Federation of Film Archives.[7]

In 1963, the comprehensive center of European photographic history—the famed Gernsheim Collection—was moved from London to Austin, Texas, following its purchase by the University of Texas. The two principal historians responsible for the collection were Helmut Gernsheim and his wife Alison, who began the work of researching, collecting, and promoting the history of photography

[6]Information on the film collection of the Library of Congress draws heavily from John B. Kuiper, Head, Motion Picture Section, Prints and Photographs Division, Library of Congress, "Opportunities for Film Study at the Library of Congress," *Film Library Quarterly* (Winter 1967–1968), 30–31.

[7]James Card, "Film Archives," *Food for Thought,* November 1959, pp. 62–63; also Charles Topshee, "What Has Canada Done?" *Food for Thought,* November 1959, p. 66.

in 1945. During two decades of intensive work they produced 12 major exhibitions in 7 countries, 19 books, and more than 150 periodical articles related to the collection.

The main strength of the collection is British photography from the earliest images in the 1830s to 1914; there is also valuable material from the United States and Europe (including the first known photographic image by Niepce made in 1826). Some material from 1914 to World War II is also available. About 30,000 original photographs, 3500 books and periodicals about photography, and several pieces of photographic equipment and apparatus comprise the three categories of collection.

There is no complete catalog available for the collection, but the publication *Creative Photography, 1826 to the Present: An Exhibition from the Gernsheim Collection* (1963) covers its scope. About a thousand items—the best of the Gernsheim's material—were shown at the Wayne State exhibit. The print collection in Austin is filed by photographer, an important asset for most historians in photography. Books in the collection are indexed on file cards by author and title. Items relating to cinema are listed in a master's thesis by David Haynes, "A Descriptive Catalogue of Filmic Items in the Gernsheim Collection," (University of Texas, 1969).

Copy photographs of prints in the collection may be purchased by researchers, and a reproduction fee is charged if a photograph from the collection is published. Inquiries about the collection may be addressed to Photography Collections, University of Texas, Box 7219, Austin, Texas.[8]

Around the country the following repositories may be of import to scholars for individual or regional studies:

Museum of Modern Art, New York—Department of Photography, Steichen Study Center, includes books and photographs primarily for twentieth century. Important collection of Atget recently acquired. Department of Film circulates its collection.

Museum of the City of New York—Fifteen albums of the photo-

---

[8]James B. Colson, "The Gernsheim Collection: A Resource for Studying the Beginnings of Photojournalism" (Paper delivered at a research session of the Photojournalism Division, Association for Education in Journalism, Berkeley, Calif., August 1969).

graphs of Jacob Riis. Prints were carelessly made some years ago from Riis plates. Pictures may be copied or prints ordered from Museum's lab. Reproduction fee charged for publication of photographs.

New York Public Library—Mixture of hand-art prints and photographs organized by subject for general picture research. Duplicate set of F.S.A. prints, though many originals loaned were never returned.

National Archives, Washington, D.C.—Photographs from all branches of government deposited here. Holds duplicate set of Brady plates made in the field, but many photographs which the Archives have are not at the Library of Congress. Important manuscripts, of course.

Smithsonian Institution, Washington, D.C.—Within the Division of Graphic Arts of Smithsonian has developed a collection on the technology of photography. Recent interest has been shown in acquisition of important photographs for exhibition and study. This small archive will certainly grow in importance to the photographic historian in years to come.

State Historical Society of Wisconsin (Madison)—Its Division of Iconography is intensively involved in the collection and utilization of the photographic image. Creative, though controversial, experimentation with methods of displaying photographs to gain overtones of meaning and juxtaposition effects is ongoing. Division headed by Paul Vanderbilt, formerly of the staff of the Prints and Photographs Division, Library of Congress.

A final, but very valuable source to the photographic historian are repositories of individual publishers. For example, the photographic library at *Look* magazine has on file contact prints, negatives, and transparencies owned by the magazine since its founding in 1937. These holdings have been carefully cataloged by subject and by photographer. Thus, it is possible to retrieve from the *Look* library citations for major contributions of any staff photographer. *Life* magazine maintains a similar archive. Because most periodicals are indexed by author (writer) rather than photographer, research on a given photographic contributor requires assists from the publisher to avoid laborious searches through each issue of the bound volumes. Most publishers' libraries have not been designed to accommodate independent researchers, so careful preparations should be undertaken to gain access to the card catalogs. A researcher would be well advised to correspond directly with the publisher's librarian.

CONCLUSIONS

Historical research on photographic communication is, for this writer, one of the most exciting kinds of work. To view the photographs of the Civil War, or documentary films of the social condition of the 1930's, videotape recordings of the great news events from the 1960s is almost to relive those periods. Each search into the archives brings new discoveries, important not only as scholarship, but also as personal experience. Perhaps it is a sudden awareness of the clothing, the architecture, the automobiles, or even the horses of a period. It may be the discovery of clouds in a photograph made when it was technologically impossible to record them. How did the photographer achieve such a feat? And every historian of photographic communication has been heard to express amazement at the kinds of images made by the pioneers; whether they worked in the 1850s or as recently as World War II.

The area of study is young; there are many frontiers, most of them new. It needs devoted young scholars to light the fire of discovery in the 1970s.

9 BROADCAST HISTORY: SOME UNRESOLVED ISSUES

Richard C. Burke

Richard C. Burke, Indiana University, is the author of *Instructional Television; Bold New Venture,* scheduled for publication in 1971.

Broadcasters, like athletic coaches, have never wanted for kibitzers. Just as a fan who watches one ball game considers himself qualified to comment on the players, coaches, and officials, anyone who sits through an evening of television feels free to generalize about broadcast programming. But exposure does not qualify as expertise, and broadcast history is something more than catchwords and generalizations such as "more radio and TV sets in American homes than bathtubs," "more hours per day spent with TV than with school," and "for news, more people depend on broadcasting than on print."

The serious broadcast scholar—the man concerned with regulation and responsibility, patterns of financial support, the impact of technology on broadcast practice, measurement of effects of television on behavior—has to prove that he is not just another dilettante. Anyone who hopes to say anything worthwhile about the development of broadcasting in this country had better come to understand some facts of life at the outset.

1. *Not many scholars are interested in broadcasting, as such.* The broadcast historian will have many acquaintances, but few colleagues. Broadcasting is of profound, if peripheral, interest to any number of economists, psychologists, sociologists and others, who examine the field *in relation to* something else; rarely will broadcasting be studied as if it had an identity of its own. The scholar uniquely interested in broadcasting, who wants to look at the field from the inside out, rather than vice versa, finds the literature sparse indeed. One radio and television department in a major university has found itself in the embarrassing position of not being able to spend all of its library allowance each year. There simply are not many books which focus on the broadcast media themselves.

2. *Although journalism has a rich history dating back several centuries, the concept of "mass media" is relatively recent.* Radio is only 50 years old and television has been significant less than half that long. There are many (although fewer than formerly) traditional historians who scoff at the idea that anything less than a few centuries old even qualifies as history. Undeniably, perspective is the stuff of history. The broadcast historian is sometimes frustrated by the nagging fear that he was born a generation too soon. Suppose, for instance, that he wants to study the relationship between print journalism and broadcasting—a fertile field in view of the patterns of cross-media ownership. Like the Federal Communications Commission, he will likely discover that the quality of print-broadcast relationships is wildly uneven and that some of the best, and some of the worst, stations are owned by newspaper publishers. The pattern, if any, may not emerge for many years.

3. *The original source material is scarce.* Although there have been some praiseworthy attempts to develop oral history collections, the stuff of broadcasting is by definition ephemeral. It is much easier

to preserve newspapers or magazines than spoken words. Only recently have systematic efforts been launched to collect, catalog, and preserve broadcast resource materials—including recordings, scripts, and business records. So far there has been more success with films than with sound recordings, kinescope, and videotape recordings. Of necessity, the broadcast historian often finds himself working with secondary sources, such as published criticism of programs or personal recollections about a program.

4. *Formulating issues for analysis is difficult.* Professor John M. Kittross of Temple University observed that broadcasters have spent most of their professional lives in glass houses, almost constantly under investigation by one or more congressional committees. That is to say nothing of all the investigations by regulatory agencies, state and local officials, the clergy, educators, citizens' groups, and courts. Apparently, these groups agree that broadcasting is too important to be left to the broadcasters. Such attention has conditioned broadcasters to be defensive and wary, if not schizoid.

Let us distinguish *philosophical* issues: the shape of the institution, its role in society, and broad matters of public policy, from *operational* issues. The operational questions are determined by structures, institutions, and practices already in existence. Examining the historical development of the FCC's position on cigarette advertising, obviously, is an operational issue; whether the government should be concerned with regulation of broadcasting at all is a philosophical question.

Perhaps broadcast historians have been too much concerned with operational questions at the expense of philosophical ones. For the past two decades, for example, we have been concerned with various aspects of subscription ("pay") television without asking about alternatives to our present system of broadcasting and how well the public would be served by them. Implicitly, we accept the premise that there will always be some agency like the FCC which will coordinate all federal activities relating to broadcasting. This simply may not be the case. We also assume, again implicitly, that there will be some sort of broadcasting system distinct from the newspaper system, but technological developments such as facsimile may make the two virtually indistinguishable.

·   ·   ·

In Newton Minow's famous "vast wasteland" speech in 1961, the FCC chairman reminded the National Association of Broadcasters that the people own the air: "For every hour that the people give you, you owe something. I intend to see that your debt is paid with service." He made it clear that the FCC should look closely at programming before renewing station licenses. While in practice little happened as a result of this threat, it does epitomize the conflict between public and private interests.

The broadcasters literally begged the federal government for regulation in the 1920s, but it was only technical matters, such as equipment specifications and frequency allocations, that they wanted regulated. They got more than they bargained for because the Federal Communications Act, while specifically prohibiting censorship by the FCC, charged the regulatory agency not only with supervision of technical matters, but also with seeing to it that the publicly owned airwaves were used to benefit the public. The FCC and the courts have agreed that *review* of a station's performance in programming during the previous three-year licensing period does not constitute censorship.

The broadcaster is told to conduct his profit-oriented business in a manner to serve the "public interest, convenience and necessity." Such concepts change constantly, leaving the broadcaster in a quandary, the FCC in a state of flux, and the public thoroughly confused. Whatever historical perspective the broadcast historian can provide will certainly be appreciated. More specifically, the broadcast historian might profitably answer such questions as the four which follow.

1. *How have definitions of "public interest" changed over the last half century?* Broadcasting began as point-to-point communication, with its financial support from the sale of receivers. The parallels with newspapers, on one hand, and public utilities, on the other, helped shape the development of its regulation. There have been FCC directives and court decisions through the years which have sought to define what it meant for a broadcaster to serve "public interest, convenience and necessity," and these could be traced. There were major changes of philosophy, for example, between the FCC directives of 1946 ("The Blue Book") on public service responsibilities and those in the 1960 revision. Even more striking were the changes during the 1960s which implied increased interest in the

rights of the viewer when they were in conflict with those of the broadcaster.

2. *What are the implications of broadcasting's big business beginnings?* Although broadcasting students groan at trying to untangle the complicated maneuvering of such giants as RCA, AT&T, and American Marconi during the early days of broadcasting, such study explains much about the shape of today's institutional structure. Even more important, it gives perspective to such recent struggles as satellite, cable, public, and pay television. It is important to understand the milieu of big business and political power in which broadcasting grew up and remains. In this respect, it is quite different from print, which developed (in this country at least) in the control of small entrepreneurs.

3. *Who has, and who should have, control access to the broadcast media?* In theory at least, the printer with his proverbial apronful of type still can set himself up in the newspaper business; the broadcaster needs permission from the government before he can start operations. The printer's performance is a matter between himself and his readers and advertisers; the broadcaster's performance is subject not only to the laws of the marketplace but also to scrutiny by the federal government. The implications of these differences are profound.

If radio and TV stations were classified as common carriers—which they definitely are not—there would be no question about access. The station's time would be sold on a first-come, first-served basis at a rate fixed by a regulatory agency. But under our system, the station owner has almost total control over who gets to use the frequency assigned to him—either for free or for pay. The national Democratic Party focused attention on this question in early 1970 when it sought unsuccessfully to purchase time on a network. The network simply did not want to sell it to them, and traditionally networks and stations have been permitted almost total discretion in such matters; however, the new spirit of emphasizing the need for public participation in current issues which prevailed in 1970 may change this. Closely related aspects of access to the media are governmental pressures on broadcasters to comply with fair employment practices for minorities and to permit minority groups to purchase media outlets.

4. *How shall broadcasters gain access to information?* In dealing

with the question of access *by* the media, as opposed to access *to* the media, we must allow for a much wider interpretation of conflict of interest because the interests in conflict are both public. Government officials interpret the public interest one way (closing a record or proceeding to public view) and broadcasters interpret it another (exposing public business to public view). Perhaps the broadcast historian can provide some perspective by showing that the relationship between government and the media always has been an uneasy one and that it probably is better that way.

An interesting manifestation of this conflict is the "television in the courtroom" issue. The American Bar Association holds that broadcasting and photographic personnel and equipment distract trial participants and demean the judicial process by distorting it. Broadcasters say the Constitution guarantees a public trial and that they represent the public every bit as much as "pencil" reporters. Further, they insist that new equipment is not distracting and does not need banks of arc lights, etc. Neither side has much solid evidence, which helps explain why the debate never has been very productive. Broadcast historians can look at results of cases which have been televised (most notably in Texas and Colorado) and look for parallels in trial coverage by other media. One case in point was the filming in 1969 of a Black Panther trial in Denver by National Educational Television. NET stations carried six hours of the case (including comments by the attorneys and judge both during and after the trial) over four successive nights.

•   •   •

There have been some studies of the trends in programming over the years, but not nearly enough. This is one type of research that is fairly simple, since it can be done with published radio and television logs. More detailed content analyses can be done where there are preserved recordings or scripts.

There also have been studies of the decision-making ("gatekeeper") processes in stations and networks, but again we need many more. The broadcast media offer fine opportunities for participant-observer studies.

Regardless of how they are structured, there is an inherent and serious difficulty with studies of broadcast content and decision-making. The central problem is that eventually the scholar is forced to deal with questions of critical judgment and personal taste. Every student of broadcasting should be familiar with at least the basic themes of the enormous literature dealing with mass culture, popular culture, and mass entertainment, but he must keep in mind that questions of taste and critical judgment do not lend themselves to rational proof. There is an extremely wide range of opinion regarding such concepts as "good" programs, "quality" programs, and the level of public taste.

In the late 1960s and early 1970s, the FCC made several efforts to diversify programming. The underlying assumption was that less domination of stations by network program control, more access by independent producers, and more local production would provide not only more diverse, but "better" programming fare. The same basic approach can be seen in the commission's attempts to diversify ownership in the broadcast media. Again, the specific features of a plan are not as important as the fact that a regulatory agency attempted to provide greater access to the broadcast media by acting on the assumption that 60 owners are better than 50 (or that 51 are better than 50, for that matter), as far as providing diversity and a wider range of entertainment, information, and opinion.

Surveys of television viewers never have found wide dissatisfaction with program offerings. In light of that, some would argue that citizens' groups intent on imposing their idea of "improved" television fare on the stations and networks were essentially antidemocratic. (A study of the rise of the militant citizen groups would make a good historical study in itself.) The same might be said of attempts by the FCC to tinker with the basic relationships among the networks, stations, and public. Others would argue that the broadcast system has obligations to serve subgroups and elites as well as the masses.

The resistance to technological innovations would make a series of good studies in broadcast history. Like any other successful businessman, the commercial broadcaster is wary of new developments which threaten his dominant position. Considering the potential for satellites and cable to diminish the need for local stations, the concern of small broadcasters over such developments is understandable. During the 1960s the big broadcasters decided that if they could not lick cable, they would join it, and by 1970, commercial broadcasters owned about 40 percent of the CATV business. This is a trend worthy of continued scrutiny by the broadcast historian.

Public television does not compete with commercial television for advertising dollars, but it does so indirectly by threatening to compete for affluent viewers. Any time a viewer is looking at public television, he obviously is not being exposed to a sponsor's commercial messages.

Like the other alternatives to commercial broadcasting, public television is worthy of more extended consideration. Here, briefly, are some of the specific problem areas of public television.

1. *What is the mission of public television?* Many critics suggest that public broadcasters always have gone after too narrow an audience with programs which are too highbrow. The ill-fated experiment with Public Broadcast Laboratory in the 1967–1968 and 1968–1969 seasons at least hinted at the potential for providing a broad spectrum of programs. "Sesame Street" a year later showed it even more clearly. Both, significantly, were financed by foundations. Public television has the potential for providing alternatives for peoples of different taste levels, different income levels, and different educational backgrounds.

2. *How can public television be financed?* Not only have public stations been underfinanced, but they have been financed on a year-to-year (sometimes almost day-to-day) basis. That kind of financial situation does not encourage bold programming which might cut off the few remaining dollars of income. The broadcast historian could look at advantages of tax, foundation, and subscription support.

3. *Should public broadcasting be national or local?* If such groups as National Educational Television and the Corporation for Public Broadcasting produce and control the content of the programming, there are obvious advantages in costs over each station producing its own. But does that not run counter to the diversity-is-good philosophy which the FCC has encouraged in commercial broadcasting?

•   •   •

Questions of responsibility, freedom of expression, public interest, access, and programming will provide unlimited opportunities for future historical scholarship.

As we look back on fifty years of broadcast history, we can see many instances where broadcasting might have developed quite differently if there had been some guidelines or policies. At last, we have begun to realize that if broadcasting is to develop its full potential in American society, we need to invest time and human resources in formulating communications policies—*before* the problems present themselves. Hopefully, scholars of the future—including historians—will devote more of their time to policy formulation.

10 LOCAL NEWSPAPERS AND LOCAL HISTORY

William H. Taft

William H. Taft, University of Missouri, is the author of *Newspapers as Tools for Historians*, *Missouri Newspapers*, and many articles for scholarly and professional journals.

Because the history of our nation is recorded daily in our newspapers, any historical account must draw on these headlines and news stories. Newsmen write for today, but what they write will form the substance of what appears in tomorrow's textbooks. Journalism frequently has been called history in a hurry.

Despite all the faults placed on the doorsteps of the nation's newspapers, they do "perform an essential function that is little understood and even less appreciated by too many of their readers," notes John

Tebbel. "It is discouraging to realize that understanding of how news is gathered, written, and transmitted is so slight that some people prefer the fantasy world of the news magazines to newspapers, or the fragmentary world of television and radio to the relative completeness of papers. Slickness and the voice of authority, whether in news magazines or television, are no substitute for substance."[1] For the researcher, the printed word so readily available from the files and microfilms of newspapers is more valuable than the hard-to-locate words of the radio-television commentators or the opinionated summaries in the news magazines.

Historians differ widely in their views on the role of newspapers in research; however, they tend to be more in agreement on their significance for researching local issues than for more complex problems with national and international implications.

Such an approach is not new. In a listing of American newspapers for 1821–1936, Winifred Gregory notes that "The value of the information which these papers contain can hardly be overestimated. They are a primary source for national and local history and for a study of the evolution of economic and political opinion . . . the record of our industrial and business history."[2]

Among the earlier advocates of the utilization of local newspapers by historians was Lucy Maynard Salmon, who provided researchers with "the most thorough-going analysis of newspaper value that has ever been undertaken" in her two books, *The Newspaper and the Historian* and *The Newspaper and Authority*. In these volumes she furnishes the reader with background data on varied journalistic practices, from the basic operations of newspapers to the complexities of the freedom of the press struggles.[3] Forty years ago, Miss Salmon recognized many of the problems associated with the use of newspapers for any historical research. Warning against either blanket accusations or universal acceptance of the press, she noted that "A

[1]John Tebbel, *Open Letter to Newspaper Readers* (New York, 1968), p. 41.

[2]Winifred Gregory, ed., *American Newspapers, 1821–1936: A Union List of Files Available in the United States and Canada* (New York, 1936), introduction.

[3]Lucy Salmon's books, published by Oxford University Press, were reviewed in an unsigned account in the *American Historical Review* 31 (1925–26), 146–148.

newspaper may be absolutely authoritative in every one of its numerous departments and yet apparently wield comparatively little influence, while another may be notorious for its inaccuracy, its misleading and even false statements, and for its unreliability, and yet it may exert an influence out of all proportion to its true worth."[4]

Such warnings need to be heeded by historians and by newsmen as well. For example, too frequently historians today automatically recommend to their students that they turn to the *New York Times* for background material. A journalism historian, on the other hand, is more aware of the history of this newspaper since its founding in 1851 and is conscious of its weak periods in the late nineteenth century. During some of these years, before Adolph Ochs took over the management of the *Times*, the *New York Sun, World, Herald, Tribune,* or *Post* would furnish researchers with a clearer and more informative picture of the metropolitan scene. For some areas today, the researchers might discover bias in the *Times*, a newspaper widely used by many primarily because of its availability in thousands of libraries and for its valuable *Index*.

At the same time, Miss Salmon observed that "The press as a whole may rise superior to its limitations and, like the historian, wrest victory from defeat."[5] To wrest victory from defeat, the historian must know the background of the newspaper he is probing, the bias attitudes of the publisher and the editors, and, if possible, the individual reporters.

Journalists and historians deal with the same basics: the record of men, their activities, their conflicts, their achievements, and their contributions to our history—local, national, and international. Both must guard against broad generalizations. What is meant, for example, by "the press"? Actually there is no such thing as "the press" or even "the American newspaper." No two newspapers are the same, even those published under the same ownership in the same community. Newspapers do not fully agree on the exact interpretation of the major events in our nation's development any more than do historians. Even the titles of newspapers can be misleading; for example, the early *St. Louis Republican* was Democratic while the *St. Louis Democrat* was Republican.

[4]Salmon, *The Newspaper and Authority*, p. 385.
[5]*Ibid.*, pp. 444–445.

James Parton, president of the American Heritage Publishing Company, noted that "Good journalists have always instinctively used the historical approach in their writing; to a lesser, but recently accelerated extent, historians have applied the techniques of good journalism to the writing of good history."[6]

Two American historians, who were pioneers in the use of newspapers as sources for their books, were John Bach McMaster and James Ford Rhodes. McMaster turned to the newspapers for essential background facts used in his *History of the People of the United States,* published in 1883. Rhodes, too, looked upon the newspapers as a valuable source to reflect the contemporary scene. More than half a century ago, Rhodes concluded that "Their object is the relation of daily events; and if their relation is colored by honest or dishonest partisanship, this is easily discernible by the critic from the internal evidence and from an easily acquired knowledge of a few external facts . . . the newspaper itself, its news and editorial columns, its advertisements, is a graphic picture of society."[7] Others have concurred, including H. G. Wells, who considered himself to be a journalist more than an historian, and Carlyle, who thought of histories as a "kind of distilled newspapers."

It hardly seemed necessary for the reviewer of Robert S. Harper's book, *Lincoln and the Press,* to observe that "the whole story of Lincoln and the press certainly cannot be found in 'the yellowing files of the newspapers themselves.'"[8] No experienced researcher nor newspaperman would expect to find all of his data within such limited boundaries. Yet there is historical gold in the yellowing files. Microfilms, now widely used by the newspaper researchers, have solved a problem recognized by Albert Bushnell in 1898, when he urged libraries to accumulate back issues even if they might require all of Manhattan Island merely for the files of the Sunday editions of the metropolitan newspapers.

"Historians simply could not do their job if it were not for

---

[6]James Parton, "The Marriage of History and Journalism," *Journalism Educator,* Fall 1965, pp. 119–125. See also Gay Talese, *The Kingdom and the Power* (New York, 1969), for an inside account of the operation of *The New York Times,* the personalities involved, and the debates over handling certain stories.

[7]James Ford Rhodes, *Historical Essays* (New York, 1909), pp. 83–97.

[8]*American Historical Review* 56 (1950–51), 914–915.

journalists," W. M. Kiplinger wrote in 1966. "The record of the times are not to be found anywhere else except in the press. Even the advertising and the commercials are rich in source materials."[9] A century ago similar comments were recorded by two writers of a history of St. Louis. "There is nothing that indicates the substantial character of a city more truly than the newspapers which start and grow up with it. They are both business and intellectual thermometers which indicate the degree of individual and general prosperity. . . . Publications reflect the sentiments, opinions, culture and tastes of our people," wrote Joseph A. Dacus and James W. Buel.[10]

Newspapers, then, play a dominant role in historical research. Although some limitations are acknowledged in any study of a community, county, or state project, the newspaper remains in the forefront in furnishing valuable data, frequently informative material not available from any other source. It is with this more limited use of the newspaper that this essay will concern itself. Much of this data has evolved from an intensive study of the newspapers in Missouri, a state with a publishing record that began in 1808 with the *Missouri Gazette*.[11]

Assuming that an individual plans to research a project involving a local or state issue, how should he make use of the newspapers? Missouri is fortunate to have its excellent State Historical Society, founded by the Missouri Press Association in 1898. These early editors and publishers, recognizing the urgent need for a central place to deposit their publications, realized how useful these items would be in compiling local historical accounts that reflect the highlights of the state's history. They had encountered numerous problems in preparing for historical talks before their MPA meetings in 1897. A history of the association's first decade was incomplete; many reports and newspaper files were missing.

So, in 1898, the newspapermen began to contribute copies of their newspapers to Columbia after the University of Missouri agreed to house these documents. More than 200 daily and weekly papers began to arrive regularly, along with other documents the publishers

[9]Letter to author, July 5, 1966.

[10]Joseph A. Dacus and James W. Buel, *A Tour of St. Louis* (St. Louis, Mo., 1878), p. 536.

[11]William H. Taft, *Missouri Newspapers* (Columbia, Mo., 1964).

printed. Most of this material has been transferred to microfilm now. In addition, the society has thousands of original editorial cartoons and for many years has been the official repository for state documents and records.

"The newspaper scatters the mists of ignorance and prejudice by flooding the pathway of man with the sunlight of truth," said a St. Joseph publisher in the first official address of the Missouri Press Association in 1868. Five years later, another prominent Missouri publisher said the press "is doing more for civilization and the cause of humanity than any other agency in the world" to enlighten, instruct, and inform the populace. Such high sounding words have been spoken by editors through the years, and they give today's researchers an idea of what the newspapermen had in mind for their publications.

In his informative book, *The Pioneer Editor in Missouri* (1965), William Lyon describes some nineteenth-century printers. The problems they encountered in the growing Louisiana Territory were similar to those faced by Eastern editors a century before and in later years along the trails of the Far West.

The pioneer editor was a public printer as well as a newspaper publisher. In this capacity he was responsible for printing the laws, proclamations, and other announcements of the officials in the territories and states. Such documents have untold value for researchers. Unfortunately, too many of these early imprints have been lost. Joseph Charless, Missouri's first printer, delayed the publication of the *Missouri Gazette* until he had printed the laws for the Louisiana Territory. Charless once said he would be the "independent guardian of the rights and liberties of the people" and looked upon his newspaper as the organ to sound the alarm should difficulties arise.

These early editors looked upon their new communities much as a mother looks upon her newborn child. For a community to succeed, it needed strong support from the newspapers. In printing glowing accounts of their new communities, the editors urged other persons with the pioneering spirit to move in. In sending exchange copies to the more established newspapers in the East, the publishers served a function now handled by a Chamber of Commerce that seeks out and offers enticing bait to new industries, settlers, merchants, bankers, and professional men.

"With little more than a shirttail full of type, an old Washington hand press, a few sheets of assorted sized paper, and an apprentice helper, hundreds of printers set out more than a century ago to inform Missourians about what was occurring in their communities, their neighboring states and territories, and the nation."[12] This scene was repeated in hundreds of communities. Each printer and his apprentice was recording American history in the making, reflecting the pioneer spirit often in words that "stretched" the truth yet expressed the voice of the grassroots populace that dreamed of the day when their own rude settlement would become the New York or Boston of the West. The researcher must be aware of such over-enthusiastic accounts, remembering that frequently they reflected more hope than fact. An editor was one of the new town's leading citizens: the unofficial greeter of visiting dignitaries, the recorder of historical highlights, the master of ceremonies on key occasions, the adviser to political and civic leaders. Little wonder then that this spirit was carried over into his writing, especially at a time when the newspapers were more the reflection of the personal views of the owners than the objective writing of today.

An editor was expected to "mould the thoughts of his constituency," as the late Walter Williams once said. Such an editor was his own master, yet he was expected to be honest, truthful, and intelligent. By direct and indirect means, the editor could sway destinies through his editorials, letters, and essays calling for action to obtain better roads, more educational facilities, improved travel connections with the nearby cities, greater use of the state's resources, and other projects of a lasting value. Today's visitors to Kansas City quickly become aware of its beautiful residential areas, the winding roads, and excellent parks; few individuals are aware of the lifelong struggle waged by Col. William Rockhill Nelson in his *Kansas City Star* for such civic projects which were deemed impractical by so many settlers in the 1880s and 1890s. Researchers, however, today can turn to the complete files of the *Star* and read thousands of words of editorial comment pointing out the urgent need for parks, benches, better residential areas, a civic auditorium, etc. In these files also can be found letters to the editors, frequently

[12]*Official Manual of the State of Missouri*, pp. 1–2.

voicing the pro and con opinions of the day. Nelson took a city of mud and turned it into a city of marble.

There are few printed sources more valuable to probe or more enjoyable to review than the files of a small-town weekly newspaper. Here the historian-researcher soon becomes lost in the past. In pursuing the editorial comments, as well as the advertisements frequently mixed in with the news accounts, he returns to past eras and finds the picture Lucy Salmon promised he would. In looking at the advertisements, he determines what the people were buying, what they were wearing, what they were paying for merchandise, what they were reading. He finds out about the thinking of the community leaders who took time to inform the readers about their views, frequently in long-winded letters to the editor. Politicians quickly recognized they could reach the mass of voters through the press. One of Missouri's first senators, Thomas Hart Benton, carefully utilized the press throughout his long political career, at times writing his own stories for local editors to print. Many of these comments are available today only in these newspaper files.

No biography could be written without newspaper files. Although Arthur Schlesinger, Jr., has been most critical of the nation's newspapers since he left the Washington political scene, he obviously had to utilize the press years ago to write his biographies of Presidents Andrew Jackson and Franklin D. Roosevelt. Without the newspapers of those years, Schlesinger would have had a void in his books. His father depended even more on the newspapers for his prize-winning volume, *Prelude to Independence* (1958).

The proper use of the community newspapers can reward the researcher with the thrill that comes from unearthing an heretofore unpublicized bit of history. Buried deep in the files of these publications are thousands of such items waiting for historians to bring them out to the light of day. As Norman A. Graebner of the University of Virginia told the Local History Enrichment Conference in 1968, historians, whether local or national, whether professional or amateur,

> are engaged in one of the world's most exciting adventures. Like all fundamental challenges to the intellect, history is concerned with the dual elements of discovery and analysis. Both elements are important, both exciting. One deals with the unearthing of

new material, one with the proper and imaginative use of that material. . . . It is amazing what can be learned from old newspapers.

He then noted some questions of universal significance about every community's history.

Why are some urban areas large and others small?

What was the pattern of transportation development?

What role did the community play in the search for better and wider markets?

What dreams of commercial greatness did the quest for roads, canals, and railroads fashion in the minds of those who promoted them?

What were the patterns of internal growth?

The answers to these questions and many others are to be found in the record of the past contained in newspaper files.

Other historians have voiced their views of the value of newspaper files. Roy F. Nichols, a past president of the American Historical Association, noted that he had "never seen a newspaper so bad that it does not contain material which could be useful to the historian." To Professor Lorman Ratner of Hunter College, newspapers are the "best source for determining the state of public opinion." Dean W. T. K. Nugent of Indiana University feels that "without newspapers we would be at a great loss to determine the simple events of the past." A balanced approach has been expressed by Professor Sidney Fine of the University of Michigan: "I should hate to have to depend on newspapers alone to reconstruct the past, but I should also hate to be without newspaper sources in undertaking the task."[13]

With these words of warning and of advice from historians, how can the researcher be assisted in the proper use of local newspapers? The historians must know more about the publications and such factors as the following in order to complete an objective study.

1. *The historical period under study.* For example, a century ago personal journalism was widely practiced. Missouri produced Mark Twain and Kansas had Ed Howe, both widely known personal journalists. Other states, too, had their recognized writers. In the last century, it was not too unusual for a re-

[13]Letters to author, 1967–1968.

porter to use his imagination to make up stories when the usual news source proved inadequate. Charles F. Browne created "Artemus Ward" while writing for the *Cleveland Plain Dealer* in the 1850s. He used the character to fill in voids in his local column.

2. *The controversy involved.* Missourians split during the Civil War, some favoring the North and some the South. Splits occurred within communities; one night Union supporters would raid a too-vocal Southern-oriented newspaper and the next night the followers of Jefferson Davis would upset a Northern-oriented publication. For a sensible use of such newspapers, the researcher must be aware of the community sentiments.

3. *The political views.* Editors were more open in presenting their political views during the last century than they are now. It was not uncommon to find on the editorial page such pronouncements as "Abe Lincoln for President." Such notices would appear in each edition for months preceding an election. These editors considered it an obligation to promote the campaign for Lincoln and to downgrade all comments against him. An excellent example of personal political writing appeared in the Lexington, Missouri, *Caucasian* in the 1860s–1870s. The title alone is adequate to attract the attention of those now probing the segregation-integration issues. The editor from 1869 to 1875 was Patrick Donan, a native Mississippian. In 1872, Donan assisted in getting Horace Greeley into the Presidential race, although earlier he had called the New York editor an "old lunatic." Donan wanted Grant out of office and referred to the President as "Ulysses Tanglefoot" and "Ulysses the Tumblebug." Donan's "Give them hell" language was directed against the North, especially New England, the radical government, and all those who surrounded Grant.[14] The researcher might wrongfully conclude that such views represented all Missourians after the Civil War unless he inquired more into Donan's background and prejudices.

4. *The mood of the people.* This will be extremely difficult to

---

[14]Lewis O. Saum, "Donan and the Caucasian," *Missouri Historical Review* 63 (July 1969), 419–450.

determine unless one probes at least two newspapers in a community, more when available. No researcher wants to rely on a single source for any information. Prior to the 1930s, one could usually find at least two newspapers in most county-seat towns, one to represent the Democrats, one the Republicans. When only one point of view is available, the researcher should turn to the leading publications in adjoining counties. It was the accepted practice of early editors to comment about activities in nearby communities. They often told of civic projects in these neighboring towns and would urge their own local leaders to emulate such projects.

5. *The bias of reporters.* This is difficult to determine in the older newspapers since bylines did not come into use until the Civil War and then only on a limited basis. In most small-town weeklies, one could assume that the editor wrote all of the editorial content. Few historians are fooled by an "Independent" tag that the publishers frequently apply to their newspapers. As noted earlier, the editor considered it his obligation to take sides in all campaigns; to be neutral was seen as the cowardly way out. An attempt to present both sides of the Civil War on the editorial page of the *St. Louis Republican* infuriated readers. The newspaper was edited jointly by a pro-Unionist and a pro-Secessionist, whose conflicting views appeared side by side; the public looked upon such efforts as a weakness and a sign of duplicity. Some even called the newspaper "the swill-tube."

6. *The sources of news.* There was a time when the editor wrote all of the news that appeared in his paper. He clipped the features from the exchanges, usually selecting those that fit into the open spaces on his pages. Others depended on local political leaders to provide the editorial comments, especially in a campaign year. The smaller weeklies also turned to the nearby city dailies for information to reprint. A few had their own correspondents in the outlying communities. The small-town dailies and weeklies devoted little space to national and international news, other than that which directly affected their own area.

7. *The location of the newspaper.* County-seat publications are

more valuable than those in other towns. They tend to carry more "official" comments, more of the news that affects the individuals throughout the county. If the county seat is also a railroad center so much the better.

8. *The audience served.* No researcher today would expect to find adequate coverage of the Vietnam War in a county weekly. This has never been a primary objective of a small-town publication. On the other hand, he can expect details about local weddings, deaths, arrests, and scandals. He can expect information about national issues, but only as they apply to the local situation.

Research techniques vary with individuals, as well as with the topics. Peter Lyon, who won the 1963 Frank Luther Mott-Kappa Tau Alpha Research Award for his biography of S. S. McClure, said in his acceptance talk:

> My research technique, which is the amateur technique, is to start the hunt for a fact in utter ignorance of all source material. One of the rules of this technique is: Take your time. Don't hurry. If you feel you're wasting valuable time, go right on wasting it. When you've taken as much time as possible, if you still haven't tracked your fact down, the moment has arrived to invoke the second rule of the amateur technique, which is: Ask the librarian. The librarian, being a professional, will know exactly where to go. He will go there in a straight line, wasting neither time nor effort. He will find you the fact you need, and you can add it to all the wonderful facts—some useful, some useless, some pertinent, some impertinent—that you found while you were blundering around in your ignorance.[15]

Lyon recalled one occasion when he was searching for nothing in particular. "I had determined just to spread my net and draw it blindly through the water, to gather whatever might be there, including nothing, if there were nothing there. But there is always something."

That last statement—there is always something—reflects the role of the newspaper in historical research. There is always something

[15]*Kappa Tau Alpha Yearbook* 19 (1965).

in every newspaper that the researcher will catch in his net. "I have always tried to wring as much pleasure out of the task as possible, for every enjoyable moment and every little triumph is inevitably balanced by the tragedies that lie in the weeds, waiting for the researcher's uncertain step," Lyon added.

In my preliminary planning for a history of Missouri newspapers it quickly became evident that some steps had to precede others, and that certain areas would lend themselves to fuller development than others. Thus three major areas were clearly established as goals that might be researched more fully. If too much time was not to be wasted, these steps were to be followed:

1. A list would be required of all of the newspapers that have appeared in Missouri since the first in 1808, the *Missouri Gazette.*

2. The role played by the press in the development of the state must be probed, seeking in a way to duplicate on a state level what Frank Luther Mott and Edwin Emery have done on a national level in their journalism histories.

3. A search for significant and interesting data about individuals who have contributed to this development of Missouri newspapers would open up new areas for research.

All researchers face the need to limit their studies. In this instance, the history was to concern newspapers. Thus radio, television, and other communications media were omitted, or mentioned only indirectly, since each of these topics deserves a study of its own.[16]

For the compilation of all the newspapers it was decided that five-by-eight-inch index cards would be most suitable; they are easier to handle in a typewriter and they can carry more data than the smaller cards. Gregory's *American Newspaper 1821–1936* was a logical starting point to provide names of publications. The Library of Congress directory, *Newspapers on Microfilm,* added more titles to the list. The bulk of the data came from two sources, Rowell's *American Newspaper Directory,* which appeared annually from 1869 to 1908, and Ayer's *Directory of Newspapers and Periodicals,* which has ap-

[16]For example, see James H. Porchey, "A Historical Survey of Broadcasting in Missouri" (M.A. thesis, University of Missouri, 1969).

peared annually since 1880.[17] All copies of these two directories were consulted, as were other lesser-known directories for assorted years around the turn of the century.

What does the historian seek of interest in these directories? Founding dates are significant, although publishers at times changed these dates. (One publisher for years has listed the starting date of his paper as being several decades before the community was founded.) Other data included the frequency of publication, political leanings, names of editors and publishers. Circulation figures were included but they were not used in this research project since many were exaggerations or guesses by the publishers who sought to impress out-of-town advertisers.

Space does not permit the enumeration of all of the problems encountered in this starting project. Since the directories generally were published by advertising agencies, there was a tendency to overplay the agency's clients and to downgrade the competition. Typographical errors were common; names of editors and publishers frequently differed in spelling from year to year. Some communities changed the spelling for their names, i.e., Peirce City became Pierce City. Editors merged their newspapers with other publications and shifted founding dates about.

With so much conflicting data, the researcher must at times make decisions on his own as to starting and ending dates for hundreds of newspapers. Ending dates especially have been difficult to determine in hundreds of the more than 6000 newspapers that have appeared in Missouri. Many publishers obviously did not know the end was so near and so they could not warn their readers. Others did not want their creditors to know the end was approaching; these men preferred to end the newspaper and leave town in the dark of the night, many to start again farther out on the frontier.

Other sources are available to the researcher in compiling such a working list of newspapers. In Missouri, two prominent editors, Walter Williams and E. W. Stephens of Columbia, published in the 1890s a monthly magazine, first called *Missouri Editor* and later *Country Editor*. Included were notes about the birth and death of

---

[17]Ayer combined 1893–1894 in one volume; however the 1969 edition was considered the "centennial," apparently basing its start on Rowell's first edition in 1869.

newspapers, usually told so briefly that they added little of historical value. One edition said "The Salem *Herald* is dead" and "The East Lynne *Index* has been born." While the researcher would prefer more data, he still is happy to learn at least this much about a newspaper. It offers guidelines for additional probing in other publications in these communities. Dozens of newspapers survived for such a brief time that their names never appeared in the annual directories. Others were included but had departed from the printing world by the time the directories were available to the public.

In addition to these sources, there are many historical publications by state, county, and city associations. These frequently quote from newspapers. Similar publications in adjoining states need to be consulted, especially for articles relating to border disputes such as those between Kansas and Missouri in the last century. Scrapbooks, collections of clippings, and diaries often contain references to newspapers.

In order to make such a list worthwhile to researchers, copies of the newspapers must be available. Through the cooperation of the State Historical Society, which published the list, data were obtained as to where copies or microfilms were available for Missouri newspapers. Information was collected from the major state, city, and local historical societies, from the Library of Congress, New York Public Library, Newberry Library, and similar centers. Since this 206-page publication appeared in 1964, additional newspapers have been located and more files have been discovered.

The response to this directory, *Missouri Newspapers: When and Where 1808–1936,* has been most favorable. The governor of Missouri called it the "most important work the Society has ever published," while the Truman Library sent a note saying "We anticipate that it will be especially helpful to use in locating material about President Truman when he was a Senator."

Although all states should have such directories, Wisconsin and Colorado are among the few others which do. They require long hours of research, patience, and tedious note-taking and typing, but they are helpful for all researchers. Along the way additional topics will become apparent for later research and articles. If one does not have the facilities nor the time to handle a statewide project, he might start with a county or a region of a state.

No historian is satisfied with producing what the layman refers to as "a list." Yet the historian realizes how such a list can serve as a guide for a fuller project, i.e., a book. Journalism researchers have found Warren Price's *The Literature of Journalism* a valuable and necessary guide. Thus it was decided that the list of Missouri's newspapers would be followed by a book, one that would reflect the role these publications have played in the state's growth and development. The smaller publications were stressed in this history, partly because there had been adequate coverage of newspapers in St. Louis and Kansas City in earlier publications.

University theses and dissertations were valuable, since history students had covered many significant elections, periods, individuals, and events. Journalism students had produced more than 500 theses and dissertations, some of which had been rewritten in book form, such as Jim Hart's history of the *St. Louis Globe-Democrat,* James Markham's biography of O. K. Bovard, and Ronald T. Farrar's study of Charles Ross.

Since 1933, the Missouri Press Association has published its monthly *Press News,* which provides much information about new and deceased newspapers, changes in ownership, and new buildings and equipment.

Many researchers will encounter a major problem that I faced. Before one can write about the state's newspapers, he first must learn the history of his state.

With these guidelines where does the researcher start? He may want to write a general newspaper history, telling the highlights and providing basic dates for significant developments in the state. He must decide what other areas he wants to incorporate with what emphasis. All of these decisions should be made before the researcher turns the first page of the newspapers he plans to use. It is too time-consuming to go back through newspapers the second time.

No state newspaper history can tell about all of the newspapers and their part in the area's growth and give adequate coverage to the personalities at the same time. After all, men and women produce our newspapers; without them the Linotypes, the presses, the computers, and other machines are of little value. In any writing, much material is left over. One can never get in all he would like to include.

Missouri has had its share of important newspapermen. It has had its pioneers, its reporters-turned-politicians such as Senator

Thomas Hart Benton. It has had some who contributed absolutely nothing; it has had leaders with the foresight to organize a press association, a historical society, and a school of journalism.

These individuals need recognition.

The skeleton for such a project already has been put together in the previous areas of research. Now a fuller study will be required to fill in the gaps about these persons. Some families will dominate, those with three- four, or even five generations involved in Missouri publishing. For more than a century one family directed a Missouri weekly; other publishing families are just beginning to establish themselves in the newspaper business.

Sources will continue to expand. County histories, which reached their peak in the 1880s, are of value if one can separate the wheat from the chaff. Individuals today appear to be more history-minded than ever before. Thus more documentary records are being maintained, old newspapers are retained, and files are sent to permanent libraries.

There is no end to this research. Before your galley proofs are back from the printers the picture has taken on new scenery. Publishers come and go; the historian seeks to keep tabs on all of them and their activities.

Much remains to be done, in Missouri as in other states. Missouri has 114 counties; only two have had their newspapers researched in detail. In addition, there are many communities with individual newspapers worth historical analysis. The specialized approaches are limitless.

All states have equally exciting newspaper histories awaiting research. It can become a lifelong chore but it will be an exciting one. And by the careful study of these newspapers, the users of the publications in the future will be better guided in their own research.

11 BEHAVIORAL CONCEPTS AND TOOLS: THE HISTORIAN AS QUANTIFIER

Robert K. Thorp

Robert K. Thorp, formerly on the faculty of the University of Kentucky and now an editor of the *Louisville Times,* is coauthor of *Content Analysis of Communications.*

There once was a journalism professor who was highly suspicious of the "new wave" of communicologists, the quantifiers, "the Chi Square Gang." His leanings were toward the humanities, and he would half-jestingly counsel his students: "You don't need to study statistics; if you need to use them, you can always hire a tame statistician."

The story might just as well be told about the traditional historian who would not dream of wedding inferential statistics, or any other quantification, with the "true" methodology of the historian.

Alas! The day of that type of historian is fast fading, and the new breed is surging to the front. Some of them are not so new, either, but they have not been much in the light until recent years. Perhaps the new historian has appeared a bit awkward, like the man stumbling about with his foot in a bucket. Indeed, the modern historian has his feet in two buckets, one labeled "traditional historical methodology" and the other, "quantification" or perhaps "heresy."

He has not been altogether awkward, this two-bucket man searching for better ways to do his job. Like any good craftsman, he has wanted to use the best tools in his work; these may be entirely traditional, or they may include sampling, statistics, computer analysis, and other instruments in the modern historian's kit.

How, then, does this new historian acquire his techniques? Certainly, he does not spring full-blown from the brow, or the person, of the traditional historian. An overnight transformation of that nature would fall under the far tail of the probability curve, or beyond. Rather, he comes to the realization slowly, or early conceives of history as at least a shirt-tail relation of the social sciences, or is steered in that direction by a problem or a professor. It follows, then, that most studies which can be classified as quantitative history are not sudden inspirations of lifelong practitioners of traditional methodology who are momentarily blinded by the dazzling new truth and converted thereby.

Some diehards to the contrary notwithstanding, the alliance—indeed the merging—of history and the social and behavioral sciences is not unnatural or sure to produce miscarriages. The reasons may be stated as follows:

> For more than a century, and especially in recent decades, much of the most precise, systematic, and sophisticated work on the motives, causes, regularities of human activity has been done by social and behavioral scientists. They have developed methods of quantification (e.g., improved methods of measurement and more sophisticated methods of statistical analysis) and of the manipulation of evidence (e.g., matrices and computers), and other methods and concepts that have permitted promising new approaches to the study of man in society. Historians necessarily have at-

tended to the results of social science and adapted their methods and concepts to historical investigations.[1]

Another historian offered this:

> In the argot of the political scientist, slightly corrupted, political historians today number an overwhelming number of standpatters, a small group of dedicated switchers, and a growing number of their new votaries. Some believe that the members of the last two categories are sufficently different from the majority of American political historians to justify calling them behavioural historians —understanding behavioural to connote, in this instance, a strong interest in the methods, results, and implications of measurement, combined with some desire to produce research that is respectable by social-science criteria.[2]

These two passages contain the kernel, but not the entire substance, of the newer approaches to historical research: measurement, quantification, statistical analysis, and all that these imply—systematic research with some controls, a certain rigor, a definite respect for the limits of inference, and the limitations of the methodology and the data.

This essay will touch on a few of these approaches, provide examples of techniques usefully applied in historical research, and point to other possible uses.

The easiest way to become acquainted with the new approaches is, of course, to take university classes, and the earlier, the better. A basic course in statistical methods will cover sampling, probability, and the simpler tests. Courses in research methods in sociology, or in some other behavioral science, will provide more on the techniques of measurement and data collection. Most universities offer "seminars" or short courses to familiarize faculty and graduate students with computer methods and possibilities, and some even have courses in, or departments of, "computer science." The latter are inclined to be mathematical.

Further, there is help. A campus computing center usually pro-

[1]Robert Jones Shafer, ed., *A Guide to Historical Method* (Homewood, Ill., 1969), p. 7.
[2]Alan G. Bogue, "United States: The 'New' Political History," in *Quantitative History,* Don K. Rowney and James Q. Graham, Jr., eds., (Homewood, Ill., 1969), p. 110.

vides advice and counsel; the higher the level of the user's sophistication, the more valuable is the advice.

But, inevitably, these questions must be answered: What is quantification? How is it useful in historical research? Is it worth the effort? The last question is important because it is presumed that any historian with a tendency to quantify will know the traditional methodology of history, as well as the newfangled. He has a choice.

"Why quantify?" is the paramount question, of course, and William O. Aydelotte, a leading practitioner of quantification in historical research, answers:

> The principal value of quantification for the study of history, stated in simplest terms, is that it provides a means of verifying general statements.[3]

All historians will generalize, some more than others, he points out, and "Quantitative methods, the numerical summary of comparable data, make it possible to avoid [the] pitfalls." Condensation "makes information easier to describe and handle" and "also helps to ensure a greater degree of accuracy."

Aydelotte points out that summaries of quantitative data

> can help to direct the student's attention to the questions most worth investigating. Since it brings the whole of the evidence, on the point it covers, into intelligible focus, the general character of the findings can be more readily perceived and relationships and differences emerge that could not so easily have been observed without the reduction of data. . . .
>
> Beyond this, a quantitative analysis offers a systematic means of testing hypotheses. It establishes how many examples there are to support each side of the argument. . . .
>
> The general overview of the whole evidence obtained by quantitative means can also be a powerful stimulus toward the reformulation of ones ideas.[4]

So quantification has uses (some examples will be given later), but what is it? It is not a game of "magic numbers," or the easy way to avoid arduous research. A computer cannot do all of the

[3]William O. Aydelotte, "Quantification in History," in Rowney and Graham, *Quantitative History*, p. 3.

[4]*Ibid.*, p. 5. Aydelotte also presents a lengthy and detailed discussion of objections to and hostility toward quantification.

work; it must be fed facts. If the facts are inferior, then the results may be disastrous. In any case, computers do not spew silken print-outs from a data deck of sows' ears.

In its simplest form, quantification is merely counting, and historians have always counted. So it could be as basic as counting the number of editorials favoring Roosevelt and/or the number against him (ignoring for the moment how the "favorable" and "unfavorable" classifications were decided). It need not involve any judgment at all, but merely "perceptual discrimination."

On a slightly higher level, there is the ranking of items (or subjects, or whatever). This might entail ranking editorials by length, Number One being the longest, say, and so on (although this particular ranking would not seem to promise much in the way of useful information). Ranking may not involve judgment, or measurement, although frequently one or the other is called for, and the quantification is escalated to higher, or more complex, levels.

Finally, there is rating, or scaling, and here the process inevitably calls for judgment, or discrimination beyond mere classification, although it may be as basic as assigning men to income groups (high, middle, low). But note that some sort of operational definitions must exist, *a priori*. The social scientist worthy of the name would set these down and follow them, rather than merely saying, "He was considered well-to-do for his time and community." (That might be a sufficient statement under some circumstances; but imprecision is not the mark of the careful researcher who would provide the facts and figures and then offer the interpretation.)

What is readily apparent is how quickly the researcher can be catapulted into a maze of problems and questions that should be answered before the research proper begins. This is part of the design stage, work done before the major task of data collection begins. Matters of quantification—measurement, statistics—are best handled early. This may be the time to call in the statistician, "tame" or otherwise, if the researcher has too little competence in research techniques to handle the problem efficiently.

Deciding what must be done in the early stages may be merely an extension of the answers given by the researcher to the questions he asks himself: What do I want to know? How am I going to find out? What am I going to do with this information (these data)? During the planning, some notion of the form of the data should emerge (the researcher, presumably, has some knowledge of the material he will be investigating; he has stated his research problem; therefore, he should know whether he will have measurements of income, favorable or unfavorable, or what). The problem and the form of the data dictate what will be done; if correlation is desired, then the material to be studied must yield data suitable for correlation (it could be age and "conservativism" of congressmen). Advice from someone familiar with the research techniques of social sciences can be invaluable here; it may mean the difference between a project that yields new data and insights and one that just adds to the accumulation of worthless "findings."

But measurement and computation do not necessarily shed light or provide insight. To the eternal comfort of the traditional historian, one of the answers to the researcher's basic questions might be that this particular problem does not lend itself to measurement, to statistics, to hypotheses, but to "crucial questions" that are best answered nonquantitatively.

Or the answer may be that this is a time for descriptive statistics (arrays of data, summaries of observations or measurements, charts), rather than inferential statistics (which would involve a sample of information from a universe of information; generalizations about the universe would be based on data extracted from the sample).

Implicit in this discussion, and in most modern research in the social and behavioral sciences, are the notions of rigor and systematic inquiry. There is a plan of research, a specified way of approaching the problem. Operational definitions are written—and followed. The researcher does not dip into his store of material, here and there, willy-nilly, until he has enough notes for a journal article; he samples systematically or he reads intensively at designated places. He does not let his impressions guide him; he defines "liberal voting record" in operational terms, and makes his judgments according to his definition. Historians have always classified; they have been less than precise—indeed, loose—in their operational definitions, and the term is not one widely used. The better the definition of categories and classifications, the better the data to be studied and manipulated.

Another mark of the scientific inquiry is the setting forth of research procedures so that the research can be evaluated or replicated. Social and behavioral scientists display their methodology, usually at the beginning of the research report—background, previous findings, theoretical considerations, methods of attack—and this may seem like a dreary recital. Then the new truth (or the old truth verified and restated, or extended) is displayed in tables, with a sometimes-gratuitous verbal translation. But the point must not be missed: The methodology is spread upon the record, where all can assess its reliability and validity (the historian appends a bibliography to demonstrate the thoroughness of *his* search).

Reliability and validity are important. Reliability means repeatability with consistency of results (using the same data universe and the same methodology, Scholar B will reach the same results as Scholar A). Validity is accomplished when the researcher measures what he says he measures (e.g., William Randolph Hearst's attitudes toward the Sixth Amendment). Demonstration of validity is often difficult; many researchers seem never to give it a thought, and in historical research, ignoring validity is easy. The researcher, whatever his field, often assumes validity while unconsciously selecting his facts to fit his prejudices—and, not surprisingly, everything usually comes out to his satisfaction.

Some attention to the problems of reliability and validity may save the researcher from gross sinning. (Such a sin is far too common to qualify as "original.") Establishing a rigorous, systematic method of inquiry for each research endeavor—and following the plan—is one aspect. Quantification seems to lend itself better to this than do the traditional methods of historical research, although historians always have concerned themselves, in varying degrees, with verification and validation. At times, quantitative techniques might aid them.

But the cause of the historian has been, primarily, to produce a narrative record, and history has been too much associated with literature to be cluttered with tiresome tables and ponderous renderings of arcane (i.e., statistical) methodology. Or so a traditionalist might argue. However, a brief methodological section is not inappropriate in a historical monograph; it could be placed near the end, which might be preferable to piecemeal presentation in footnotes or within the text. Tabular and other statistical data can be presented where appropriate; after all, they may be the substantive basis of the article or monograph.

But abstract discussions and study of techniques are worthless without some guidance to the kinds of problems amenable to quantification. One of the basic ways is to use the statistical record.

Voting behavior in the United States has been studied, often intensively, from the precinct level on up. For recent years, voting statistics are relatively easy to obtain, and political scientists use them to study trends and bellwether precincts. One historian used them to set the record straight on voting trends in the Jacksonian Era (often a loose term). What he found was that eminent historians—Charles and Mary Beard and Arthur Schlesinger, Jr., among them—had been perpetuating error in writing of the huge numbers of voters in the elections of 1824 and 1828.[5]

McCormick, of course, was just using "common sense" and good historiography; but the records proved his point.

Primary sources usually are superior to secondary, especially when the primary is an official record. By the same reasoning, a man's behavior may be considered superior to his words, although behavioral scientists and historians consider verbal activity part of behavior; and sometimes it is the only behavior to be studied. But some forms of verbal behavior are preferable to others.

Every good newspaper reporter knows that what a man says may be one thing and his actions something else. Historian Alan G. Bogue has reminded his colleagues of the same thing: "historians frequently have been more impressed by what our subjects have said than by what they have done."

Looking at two different records also changed the picture usually presented of one of this country's most famous editors, Henry Watterson. Watterson, for 50 years the outspoken editor of the *Courier-Journal* in Louisville, appears in most accounts as a fiery liberal and a champion of the Negro. This position cannot be supported except by secondary sources: his autobiography and some editorials recalling his earlier stands on behalf of the black population.

But the primary record of Watterson's behavior, his editorials dealing with "the Negro question," present a different image.[6] An "impressionistic" approach to the Watterson editorials for 1868–1872,

[5]Richard P. McCormick, "New Perspectives on Jacksonian Politics," in Rowney and Graham, *op. cit.*, pp. 372–384.

[6]Robert K. Thorp, " 'Marse Henry' and the Negro: A New Perspective," *Journalism Quarterly* 46:3 (Autumn 1969), 467–474.

for example, could have resulted in one of three conclusions: Watterson was a champion of the Negro; Watterson favored keeping the Negro in his place; Watterson vacillated and shilly-shallied on the issue. Closer scrutiny revealed the truth; sampling would have made the task easier.

Fortunately, there are a number of reliable sampling procedures for dealing with newspaper content, and others for studying other written material. Most books on content analysis include a section on sampling.[7]

Donald Shaw found sampling useful in his study of the decline of bias in Wisconsin newspapers.[8] His alternatives were to read every issue of every newspaper for his period; to select only a few and let them represent all newspapers; to take the newspapers available and sample; or to study one newspaper intensively and apply the findings to all the state's newspapers. The last would have been foolhardy; the first, impossible.

In addition to sampling, Shaw had to devise a means of measuring bias, not so complicated a task as some of the measurements invented by social scientists in their quest for deeper understanding of human behavior. Historians might adopt some of the less suspect of the techniques of measurement; there might then be more meaning to their statements of "intensity" of opinion and attitudes, or the "shrillness" of the headlines and the arguments, or "the campaign was getting hotter, and Smith's invective became harsher and more frequent." Content analysts have grappled with the problems of intensity and direction (favorable-unfavorable statements, for example), and some of their work might be useful to historians interested in verification.

For the historian who finds it necessary to refer to "shrill" headlines, "sensationalism," "yellow journalism," and other ill-defined or undefined phenomena that seem to call for adjectives, little help is available from the quantitative approach. One admonition stands out: The careful scholar defines his terms and makes them opera-

[7]Richard Budd, Robert K. Thorp, and Lewis Donohew, *Content Analysis of Communications* (New York, 1967). Chapter 4 covers sampling, and a bibliography directs attention to a broad range of material on the subject; Chapter 5 deals with measurement; Chapter 7, with direction.

[8]Donald L. Shaw, "News Bias and the Telegraph: A Study of Historical Change," *Journalism Quarterly* 44:1 (Spring 1967), 3–12, 31.

tional where possible. But attempts to measure sensationalism have not been too fruitful,[9] and the best approach may be to describe behavior rather than merely applying a label.

Another problem that frustrates historians is that of proving authorship. Here the knowledge of statistics and access to a computer are invaluable, as recent scholarship has demonstrated. There are a number of good examples of literary detective work, and even whole books devoted to the subject.[10] A determined statistician decided that James Madison was the principal author of several of *The Federalist* numbers earlier attributed to Alexander Hamilton. The question may have been decided earlier, at least to the satisfaction of many scholars; but his persistence and conclusions point up the value of statistical tools and support the other, nonquantitative arguments favoring Madison as the author of the disputed essays.

Simpler approaches also can yield rich data and may be akin to techniques common to history. One of these is content analysis, which, in the social sciences, includes a broad array of measurement, statistical methods, and classification ("content categories"). On less sophisticated levels, historians always have been content analysts, but generally less systematic and rigid than the modern approaches and certainly less inclined to take advantage of the additional data provided by even the simplest forms of quantification.

A special kind of content analysis, contingency analysis, attempts to uncover the association structure of a "message source," that is, what ideas are related in a writer's thinking. Contingency analysis can be tedious work; a well-disciplined corps of assistants is recommended.

Finally, the modern historian has much to learn from the development of techniques for ascertaining public opinion.

> Although an historian working on a 16th century problem cannot conduct a public opinion poll, an examination of questions used by modern pollsters to elicit certain types of information may suggest questions for which the historian might seek answers from old documents. A knowledge of modern sampling techniques may

[9]Percy H. Tannenbaum and Mervin D. Lynch, "Sensationalism: The Concept and Its Measurement," *Journalism Quarterly* 37:3 (Summer 1960), 381–392.

[10]Jacob Leed, ed., *The Computer and Literary Style* (Kent, Ohio, 1966).

help in the weighing of data. At the very least, these types of knowledge of modern methods will force the historian to define more carefully the concept of public opinion.[11]

Interviewing is not confined to the public opinion polls, of course, and the historian will find a considerable body of literature on interviewing techniques, based on field work and experiments in psychology, psychiatry, sociology, anthropology, and the other branches of the behavioral sciences. Considering that historians do get much information from live human sources, the modern researcher should not be ignorant of the arts and skills necessary to cope with this aspect of investigation.

Long before now there have been anguished cries that the new methodology of history will take all the blood and juices out of those beautiful narratives so laboriously, lovingly, and, perhaps, artfully constructed.

Not so. The purpose of any research technique is to add to, not detract from, the material an author acquires as the basis for his writing. If quantification provides a precise summary of vast amounts of information, so much the better; there will then be more space for beautiful prose. Nothing in quantitative methodology forbids the researcher to take notes to illustrate what he finds, to put "flesh and blood on the bones of history."

Other detractors seem to worry that "the individual case" will be overlooked if quantitative methods are used. A great many quantifiers worry about the individual case, too; they are concerned lest the individual case be so odd that it catches the researcher's fancy, enticing him to use it to the exclusion of overwhelming data to the contrary which may be lost among copious notes—or in a head full of "impressions."

The quantifiers look at the individual case in this way:

> It is a paradox of some magnitude that those historians who use quantitative methods should be criticized by those who do not on the basis that the "individual" is lost in statistics: an individual detail—whether it is part of what we know of a person or an event—is frequently represented more exactly and uniformly in quantitative history than it is in the nonquantitative varieties of the discipline. For example, the vote of a single congressman on

[11]Shafer, *op. cit.*, p. 8.

a specific issue may, in fact, be more carefully accounted for by statistical methods than by any approach which deals with politics at the level of concepts—"Jacksonian" or "Populist," for example—or of personalities, such as "hardliners" or "liberals."[12]

What should be thoroughly understood is that the quantitative methods are not advocated as the *only* ways. It is difficult to imagine that traditional approaches will lose their utility. The newer methods are alternatives to be used when the problem demands. Knowledge of them should help the historian to utilize them and to draw on the vast body of data and knowledge being accumulated by sociologists, political scientists, and even modern geographers.

This is not an either/or proposition. Aristotle is dead.

Aydelotte offers a good summing-up:

> When all reservations have been made, quantification has still shown itself, in the light of the considerable experience we now have, to be a powerful tool in historical analysis. It helps to make work both easier and more reliable, and, in some cases, it provides a means of dealing with questions that could not be attacked in any other way. Those wrestling with problems for which this approach is appropriate can ill afford to dispense with it. In the general intellectual twilight in which historians are condemned to spend their lives, even some small effort to render the darkness less opaque may be advantageous.[13]

[12]Rowney and Graham, *op. cit.,* p. viii.
[13]Aydelotte, *op. cit.,* p. 22.

71 72 73 74   7 6 5 4 3 2 1